Richmond Public Library

D A T E   D U E

MAR 28 1996
JUN 17 1998
APR 2 2 2000
JUN 11 2009

DATE DUE			
JUL 25 78			
SEP 76 78	AUG 0 9 1991		
OCT 2 6 1978			
MAY 2 1979	FEB 1 8 1993		
MAR 1 1980	OCT 2 8 1991		
JUN 9 1980	APR 0 6		
JUN 2 6 1982			
APR 3 0 1984			
NOV 1 1984			
JUN 2 4 1986			
DEC 4 1997			

Richmond Public Library
Richmond, California

THE LIBRARY OF GREAT PAINTERS

ROUAULT

LIFT COLORPLATE FOR TITLE AND COMMENTARY

8 759.4
c. 1

GEORGES
ROUAULT

TEXT BY

PIERRE COURTHION

Georges Rouault

RICHMOND PUBLIC LIBRARY
RICHMOND, CALIFORNIA 94804

THE LIBRARY OF GREAT PAINTERS

HARRY N. ABRAMS, INC., *PUBLISHERS*, NEW YORK

Library of Congress Cataloging in Publication Data
Courthion, Pierre
Georges Rouault.

  (The Library of great painters)
  Translation of Rouault.
  Bibliography: p.
  Includes index.
  1.   Rouault, Georges, 1871-1958.   I.   Courthion, Pierre.
ND553.R66C6313   759.4   76-53575
ISBN 0-8109-0459-4

Library of Congress Catalogue Card Number: 76-53575

Published in 1977 by Harry N. Abrams, Incorporated, New York
All rights reserved. No part of the contents of this book may be
reproduced without the written permission of the publishers
Picture reproduction rights where applicable reserved by S.P.A.D.E.M., Paris
Printed and bound in Japan

CONTENTS

COLORPLATES

ROUAULT

1. *The Little Port, with Figures*. 1913. Watercolor and colored pencils, 8 x 12¼". Private collection

Georges Rouault

In 1897 Georges Rouault, the son of a Belleville cabinet-maker, was a pupil of Gustave Moreau at the École des Beaux-Arts in Paris. In that year he painted a *Night Landscape (The Workyard)* in which, for the first time, his remarkable talent asserted itself with its full vigor and strength (colorplate 3). "You are Shakespeare's fellow countryman," Moreau told him as he looked at his pupil's work. This astonishing painting is filled with scaffoldings, smoke clouds, and gloomy cumulous masses; in the foreground a mysterious struggle takes place in the midst of a crowd of men and horses.

What stormy episode in the life of a workers' suburb can this watercolor, which the artist has heightened with pastel, represent? A revolt of laborers at a construction site? Butchers fighting during that year's strike by the workers at the La Villette slaughterhouses? We do not know. But the painting already reveals the essence of Rouault's talent: a sharp sense of the tragic, a spontaneous compassion for human suffering, a gift for suppressing small details that express nothing.

Rouault was twenty-six. Born in Paris in the rue de la Villette, on May 27, 1871, to the sound of the guns of the Commune, he had spent his childhood on the heights of La Courtille, in the old quarter of Belleville. Attracted by the language of colors, he had served an apprenticeship to a stained-glass artist who restored old windows. After each day's work he would set off at a run, hurrying to reach the other bank of the Seine, where he took evening art classes in which he drew from plaster casts. Thus his admission to the École des Beaux-Arts in the rue Bonaparte had been an event of great importance to him, all the more so because he studied there under an exceptional master—who was there only by a stroke of good fortune—and had as classmates Matisse, Marquet, Manguin, Paul Baignères, Evenepoel, René Piot, Bussy, Lehmann, and other promising young students.[1]

Rouault lived in a world apart, an inner world of uneasy fervor permeated by the tragic sense of life. His teacher, Gustave Moreau, who had moved beyond the symbolism then loathed by the orthodox, had helped him to see that the momentarily overrated official art had no future. It mattered little to him, therefore, that in the year 1897 Paris was filled with statues that should have been stored in old warehouses, that Léon Bonnat received a gold medal for his wretched daubings, that the members of the Académie des Beaux-Arts rose that year like outraged fathers to protest the installation in the Musée du Luxembourg of works by Manet, Monet, Degas, and Renoir—and by Cézanne, whom Rouault revered. He knew what to think of all that.

Rouault had already failed twice to win the Prix de Rome. The first time the jury declared his *Ordeal of Samson* inadequate (colorplate 2); the second time, in spite of the efforts of Gustave Moreau, the work submitted by a pupil of Bonnat named Larée was preferred to Rouault's *Dead Christ Mourned by the Holy Women*. It is true that, in compensation, Rouault had meanwhile won second prize in the Fortin d'Ivry competition in 1894 with his *Coriolanus in the House of Tullius* and, in the same year—after a protest by his fellow students caused an earlier judgment to be reversed in his favor—the Prix Chénavard with his *Child Jesus Among the Doctors*.

After the second Prix de Rome competition, Gustave Moreau had urged his favorite pupil to abandon the insidious competitions of the École and to work independently. Later Rouault came to show Moreau the paintings he had done outside of class. "They are failures, I shall have to

---

1. Moreau had come to the École to replace Elie Delaunay, who was ill.

2. *The Child Jesus Among the Doctors*. 1894.
Oil, 64⅝ x 51⅛″. Musée d'Unterlinden, Colmar

3. *The Discus Thrower*. 1886. Drawing.
École Nationale des Arts Décoratifs, Paris

begin again," he said modestly as he held them out to his master. But, having seen them, Moreau replied, "One hardly needs to thank you for what you are doing, for you yourself do not know." Thus, from the beginning, the master recognized the important role played by intuition in his pupil's talent.

But on April 18, 1898, Gustave Moreau died of cancer of the throat. His studio was at once "excommunicated," for at the École, that antechamber of the worst kind of academicism and of the fatuous conventionalism of the Académie des Beaux-Arts, there was no thought of replacing a teacher so little in line with the school's doctrine. Overnight Rouault was confronted with harsh reality. Abruptly, he was made aware of the excesses of intellectualism in which his master had indulged. From now on Rouault would be entirely cut off from the ivory tower. For this pensive boy, who had entered into the pursuit of art as others enter a monastery, this sudden loss meant the abyss, poverty. Since his family had for the time being left Paris for Algiers, it also meant that he was alone, completely on his own.

What should he do? Continue to paint the acceptable seraphs that had won him—although not without difficulty—recognition from the official teachers at the École? Or throw himself wholeheartedly into the pursuit of

that art of shadows, of that irresistible vision that he could feel growing distinct within himself?

In 1901 Rouault decided to risk all to gain all. Thus he joined Antonin Bourbon, another disciple of Moreau, who was a lay brother at the Benedictine abbey of Liguge, located in the Vienne *département* near Poitiers. Joris-Karl Huysmans, author of the virulent *Là-Bas*, who had now turned penitent, had been living for two years at the Maison Notre-Dame at Liguge. He planned to found a community of artists there, away from the frivolities of Parisian society— *le Tout-Paris*, which a Montmartre wit nicknamed the "perished society" *(le Tout-Pourri)*. In addition to Huysmans, Rouault made the acquaintance at Liguge of Forain, a man much older than himself who was trying to revive his talent, which had been dissipated by drawing for the press. The monks, however, were driven from their monastery by the absurd law forbidding religious communities in France that was brought in by that "Père Ubu" of anticlericalism, Émile Combes. Rouault, along with Huysmans and the others, had no choice but to leave.

At Liguge Rouault had been able to meditate on the value of contemplation. "Dreaming is dangerous," he wrote. "Sleep sometimes means death. But loving and constant

4. *Mother and Child*. c. 1900.
Drawing, small format.
Whereabouts unknown

5. *Study for Coriolanus in the House of Tullius*. 1894.
Drawing tinted with gouache, 18½ x 14⅝". Private collection, Paris

effort is in my view never as pointless as it appears to be to the men of action, who consider it a waste of time to fold one's arms or close one's eyes for a moment so as to see some imaginary composition take shape."

Once again Rouault faced difficult times. But in this new crisis a small stroke of luck came his way. On January 14, 1903, the Musée Gustave Moreau was opened in the rue de La Rochefoucauld, Paris, and he was appointed curator. A salary of two hundred francs per month now left him without too many worries, enabling him to continue his researches, no matter how disrespectful of conventional standards these might be. His models? Did he need any? He was imaginative, and it was enough for him to see and understand, and so to paint—in an art burning with truth, an art that seemed to be painted in his own blood—the derelicts of the Parisian slums. In his writings too, Rouault described these people who "work without respite until death" and "wounded, accept suffering courageously, admirably. No fine phrases—they *don't talk* (they don't know how), they *don't write....* They are not distinguished, and they smell of sweat. They are often ordinary to look at; they are *beautiful;* they *pray....* They pray, of course, through their actions."[2]

2. Georges Rouault, *Pages sceptiques: de la Béatitude des ventres pleins et des cerveaux vides*, catalogue of the Drouot sale, June 11, 1956.

It was at this time that he met Léon Bloy, that prophetic novelist whom Barbey d'Aurevilly used to compare to a cathedral gargoyle spewing rainwater upon the just and unjust alike. Rouault had read two of Bloy's works, *La Femme pauvre* and *Le Désespéré*. The "ungrateful beggar," as Bloy was nicknamed, confirmed Rouault in his outraged opposition to the unjust inequality whose ravages he saw all around him. Yet, to maintain friendly relations with Bloy, Rouault had to be always on his guard, for, while the refractory writer had greatly admired the pictures painted by Rouault at the École, he was soon put off by the bold experiments which followed—even though they were akin to his own. In art Bloy preferred bad painting to good; he was more of a *Dépendent* than an *Indépendent*. Nonetheless, the two shared common ground, and there was a fortuitous sympathy between them—for example, Bloy planned a book in which he would show, "to the astonishment of mediocre souls, the miraculous complicity that exists between the Holy Spirit and that most lamentable, despised, and soiled of human creatures, the prostitute."[3]

The theme of the prostitute preoccupied Rouault during the same period, just as it had already haunted Dostoevski

3. Georges Rouzet, *Bloyana*, 11ᵉ Cahier de Rhône, Neuchâtel, 1944.

13

6. *Mother and Child (The Clown's Wife)*. 1905.
Oil and gouache, 6¼ x 4¾".
Private collection, Winterthur

8. *Salome*. 1901.
Charcoal and pastel, small format.
Whereabouts unknown

7. *Paris*. 1891.
Drawing, small format.
Whereabouts unknown

9.   *Mother and Child (Madame Baignères and Her Son)*. 1906.
Watercolor, 8¼ x 6¾". Collection Mr. and Mrs. John Hay Whitney, New York

and Baudelaire. Like his friend Jacques Maritain, Rouault seems to have seen the so-called "daughter of joy" as a "sacrificial victim," the "ransom of the bourgeois order," and, in the phrase of Charles Journet, as "a mirror-image, but in despair, of the poverty of the saints."

For Rouault did not believe either in "sensible people" or in those who in his time were called "thinkers." Everything in him rebelled against facile culture and its ready recourse to clichés. His escape from the usual deadening round of studies in the sanctuaries of Italy only made him react all the more strongly against idolatrous attitudes toward certain works of art from the past falsely consecrated by custom. He

knew that the works that mark the stages in the development of earlier art were made by revolutionaries whose idiosyncrasies have been smoothed over by the passage of time. Of all the *fin de siècle* traditionalists, only Gustave Moreau had found favor in his eyes. He recognized that in the case of Moreau it was as if several painters had met head-on in one man, and that his master's intrinsic painterly power had often deviated toward a love of luxury, of antiquity, and of the goldsmith's art (the excess of gold in his pictures had caused Degas to say that Gustave Moreau had "festooned the gods of Olympus with watch chains"). But Moreau himself foresaw that he would soon be surpassed by the

10. *Punch*. 1906.
Oil and watercolor, 17⅜ x 13″. Private collection

11. *The Red Clown*. 1903.
Watercolor, 11 x 9″. Formerly collection Girardin

generation of Fauves, which he had more or less consciously encouraged and prepared. "I am the bridge," he used to tell his pupils, "the bridge over which you will pass."

Yet, for all this, Rouault was not at all a partisan of anti-culture. His art always avoided those two fallacious extremes—the strict, literal imitation of nature and the coerced rigidity of an abstraction systematically pushed to mechanical, robot-like extremes. His profound intuitive feeling for things and for people was always equally as important to him as any conceptual knowledge of them. And so whatever his eyes saw in the narrow streets, in the squares, and on the fairgrounds was transfigured by his art. His prostitutes have nothing erotic or vulgar about them; they are not the sisters of those of Degas or Toulouse-Lautrec. Rouault catches them in front of the mirror—in their moments of solitude when they perceive for an instant, with a numb sorrow, what lies behind their reflections. But which of us, the painter asks himself, does not hide behind our makeup? Contemplating the prostitutes, the clowns, the cashiers of a traveling circus, and the nightclub dancers in their grinding poverty, he felt a disgust rising up within himself and a pity for the well-to-do, the avaricious—the rich who live hypocritically, trying to forget the masks they wear.

And then there was justice—the law as it is often construed by the well-born individuals authorized by society to judge between good and evil. Rouault was too clearly aware of the difficulties of a magistrate's job not to be disturbed by its arbitrariness, so he painted lawcourt scenes to which Deputy Public Prosecutor Granier gave him firsthand access. The painter could never forget the capriciousness of the judgments that he saw being made, which the court clerk recorded in antiquated language. He put himself in the place of defendant, lawyer, and judge in turn; he saw them, and he gave them all the same bloated faces.

No other painter of his time pored over these blemishes on the face of society. None used drawing and color as he did to reveal to us, without acrimony, our unfathomable existence. At the risk of being taken for a malcontent, he braved the taste of the Joseph Prud'hommes of the period with his "masculine and severe" art. "If they had known," he wrote, "that I was baptized at Saint-Leu de Paris, the parish of Villon and of his old mother, whom he loved, it seems ...there would be no stopping them from saying, 'He is destroying everything; he is a barbarian!' They didn't realize that I am absurdly scrupulous, especially about works that no longer belong to me."

What predecessors did Rouault have for this way of painting the transcendent side of reality? Certainly not Courbet, with his crude realism whose substance is sublime but has no metaphysical background. Nor is he, to my mind, any more

12. *Dancer (At the Tabarin)*. 1906.
Watercolor and pastel. Whereabouts unknown

13. *Bal Tabarin (Dancing the Chahut)*. 1905.
Watercolor and pastel, 27⅝ x 21¼".
Musée d'Art Moderne de la Ville de Paris

closely related to Millet and his edifying peasantry, seen through the eyes of a country priest. It is rather with the socialist Daumier and his realist vision of the streets and of human manners that I would find Rouault's most frequent affinities, at least in France. In addition to their feeling for the monumental, the two artists shared a technique in which sweeping brushstrokes establish, place, and sketch out a character—boxer, clown, workingman, tramp, judge, lawyer—to whom they sometimes give their own manner and expression. Where Daumier, however, confined himself to the secular feeling of brotherhood, to what one poet has called an "infinite love for the Republic," Rouault went further. He is akin to Goya in his awareness of the dramatic and in his recognition of the spirit of evil; but where the frightening genius of that painter of tortures follows the bestiality of human beings to its most ferocious extremes, the Parisian painter remains more generously open to grace. In the disinherited people that he depicts for us there can be seen glimmering the persistent light of redemption. The whole of his work seems to offer a visual commentary on that tragic cry of Léon Bloy: "The great sorrow is that of not being saints!" The realism of Rouault is realism *transcended*.

For Rouault the decisive encounter with another artist was with Rembrandt, whose works he fervently studied in the albums of reproductions in the library of the École des Beaux-Arts. In Rembrandt's art he found a generosity and

spirituality that answered his own. Three centuries before his own time, in an era when "finish" was obligatory, Rembrandt had refused to concern himself with the vision and taste of the Amsterdam bourgeoisie and had dared to paint freely, to paint with "mud," to paint ugliness without omitting those illuminations that broke in from above upon his gloomy darkness. Surely Rouault was thinking of him when he wrote at various times in his life: "Light is tragic!"

The change of direction that suddenly occurred in Rouault's art after the death of Gustave Moreau jolted defenders of the traditional poetics even more powerfully than had Impressionism in its time, and was not unlike Van Gogh's abrupt about-face after his period of study. There was a new generation, tired of an art that had accepted without question too many mannerisms from the formalism of the past, and Rouault, like a true primitive, opened the eyes of that generation to the barbarous and the spontaneous. Unconsciously forgetting what he had been taught, he rejected false order and humdrum brushwork in favor of full subjectivity. Instinctively repudiating the theory of the German Alexander Baumgarten, who treated aesthetics (he invented the term) as an inferior kind of gnosticism on the ground that its object is not subject to deductive reasoning,[4] Rouault admitted that the pathways of art are often hidden

4. Alexander Baumgarten, *Aesthetica*, 1750.

14. *The Salon (At the Theater)*. 1906.
Watercolor, 28¾ x 21¼".
Collection Baronne Lambert, Brussels

15. *At the Café*. c. 1906.
Watercolor and gouache, 9½ x 12¼".
Private collection

behind a mysterious mist until a gleam from some secret source suddenly pierces the veil. One winter day, after a walk, Rouault told Jacques Maritain "that he had just discovered, while looking at the fields covered with snow in the bright sunlight, how to paint the white trees of springtime."[5]

As is apt to happen with artists who have a strong sense of the tragic, Rouault thirsted for amusements. A spirit of extravagant fantasy filled the sketches that he made for his own relaxation—he called them his *grotesques*—and distracted him from his major preoccupations. As early as 1910 he began to collect these phantasmagoria into albums, and sometimes in the evening he would show selections from these drawings to Jacques and Raïssa Maritain, who at about this time became his neighbors when he moved to Versailles.

Rouault's inclination toward exaggeratedly large heads and caustic wit can be found earlier in history in Pompeiian painting; it causes Callot to give his hired assassins their bristling plumes and enlivens the portraits of Goya who, as Rouault said, "gave such faces to some of the great Spanish officials of his time that we cry out with delight at the sight of their real humanity."

The Rouault of the grotesques has been compared with Rabelais and with the antics of Gargantua. For my part, I see him as more closely related to the artists of the cathedral

sculptures and to the distortions, deformities, and comic effects that they nestled in the niches beneath their tympana.

The American collector John Quinn possessed a series of these grotesques, conceived by Rouault between 1910 and 1918. These sketches were executed mainly in watercolor, with retouching in three kinds of chalk. In them *The Judge* appears as a frightened creature, *The Man with the Cigar* as a show-off, *The Prophet* as an itinerant musician. From the monumental profile of *The Superman* as a Prussian officer to that of *The Fop*, there is a whole procession of these types.

Rouault's mockery was not guided by any feeling of superiority. As the father of four children (Geneviève, Isabelle, Michel, and Agnès) he often questioned whether he had the right to pursue his uncertain and materially unproductive way of life. His compassionate laughter was never malicious. "My art is not based on exaggeration," he stated, "and I fear that accusation more than anything. I agree that the grotesque and the tragic exist cheek by jowl in my works, but surely they are as closely joined in life."[6]

After 1918 the grotesque became rare in the work of Rouault. It now appeared only as an exception, in the form of clowns and Punches. It is true, however, that in 1932 he produced a kind of recapitulation of all his grotesques in the etchings and woodcuts that he made as illustrations for *Les Réincarnations du Père Ubu*. His dealer and publisher,

5. Jacques Maritain, *L'Intuition créatrice dans l'art et dans la poésie*, Paris, 1966.

6. Statement made to Jacques Guenne, *Les Nouvelles littéraires*, November 15, 1924.

16. *Nude with Arms Raised*. c. 1906. Sketch. Whereabouts unknown

17.   *Judges*. 1908. Oil, 29½ x 41⅜". The Royal Museum of Fine Arts, Copenhagen

Ambroise Vollard, provided the text for the volume, which he had printed in the finest Elzevir type. It is a text of which the kindest thing one can say is that it is unreadable.

While he was still living at Versailles, Georges Rouault painted his own image in *The Workman's Apprentice* (colorplate 1). This self-portrait marks the first stage in the development of a theme that became dear to him and that he explored in the years that followed—the theme of human suffering. Rouault always considered himself as above all a manual worker, a laborer, a descendent of those jobbing workers who in earlier times had built the cathedrals. While his period at Ligugé had shown him the necessity of establishing a balance between action and contemplation, he also understood that to live harmoniously and produce work that is valid a man must achieve a just blend in his work of hand, mind, and heart. Furthermore, he could never forget what had been the greatest difficulty in his life—the struggle required for a man like him, who came from a world of honest workingmen, to free himself from the powerful

stranglehold of money. Having chosen to work freely in poverty rather than to gain a prosperity made possible by submission to the standards of others, Rouault concentrated in his paintings on "the hard trade of living" that is the lot of the simple people, the poor, the oppressed, and the disinherited in order to show their life, their travail, and their extreme poverty. Using blues, browns, and blacks—a palette free from excessive showiness—in works that are plain and strong, scored with bold, thick brushstrokes, he depicted their tired bodies, stooping almost to the ground; the old mother as she lugs on her back the wood that is necessary to keep her family warm; the exodus of homeless families along the frozen road.

Like the son of the Miller of Leyden, this cabinetmaker's son had a sense of community and possessed the gift of expressing it in his art. And so Rouault, like Rembrandt, sometimes gave his own features to the people he painted—a fact that brings them closer to us and prevents us, as spectators, from being cut off from the scene; we participate in it through the artist's image. And yet Rouault

18.   *Judges*. 1901. Wash, 4 x 3⅞″.
Private collection, Paris

19.   *Judge*. 1937. Oil, 24⅜ x 18⅛″.
Private collection

20.   *The Provincial Trial*. 1938. Oil, 40 x 25⅝″. Private collection

touches us not so much through the subject of his picture (which, though by no means an afterthought, remains on the whole subordinate) as through its purely painterly content in which the workman and the artist are, at some indistinguishable point, united. Infusing the pigment with his passion—one might even say with his lifeblood—he transfigures it, bringing before our eyes his joy or sorrow, his humanity, and above all, his faith. It is a faith marked by a respectful modesty, a disinclination to inscribe every patch of canvas with the image of that Divine Being who was always his ultimate model.

Rouault's painting gives itself without reservation to anyone who is willing to see it—it radiates outward. This explains the universal appeal of this man so imbued with tolerance; it explains the fact that his art is as well understood by laymen and atheists as it is by religious minds.

One day I asked Rouault the question I had already asked Matisse: "If you were cut off from your fellowmen forever, condemned to live on a desert island until you breathed your last breath, and you knew that your art would never again be

21. *The Hovel*. c. 1913.
Gouache, ink, tempera, and pencil, 12¼ x 7½".
Musée d'Art Moderne de la Ville de Paris

22. *The Poor Family (Exodus)*. c. 1911. Oil, 25⅝ x 19⅝". Musée de l'Annonciade, Saint Tropez

23. *Fugitives (Exodus)*. 1911. Pastel and gouache, 17¾ x 23⅝″. Kunsthaus, Zurich

24. *Motherhood (Run-down Faubourg)*. 1912.
Gouache and pastel, 7⅛ x 11″.
Musée d'Art Moderne de la Ville de Paris

seen by anyone, would you go on painting?" Matisse's answer had been no. Rouault's was this: "Of course I would go on; I would have need of that spiritual dialogue."

It is clear that Rouault did not think of painting as "an end in itself and for itself. . . ." For him the work of art was, as Jacques Maritain said, "good in relation to something beyond itself." The *beautiful*—that word which, fortunately, we no longer spell with a capital letter—was not limited for Rouault to the pleasing, the graceful, the pretty, the hedonistic; it encompassed all the feelings, including the terrible and the terrifying, that affect the human soul. In mid-February 1946 Rouault wrote to me, "I belong to a much older generation—to a vanished time when those who pretended to uphold the established concept of beauty would excommunicate you from the Grand Salon." For Rouault, however, art was not a game, a distraction, a luxury intended only to provide relaxation for some wealthy Croesus. It offered the painter the possibility of communicating with other men through drawing and color, through pigment that the artist has kneaded and worked; it was an outpouring of the heart, the unfolding of a secret launched into space and time, a form of prayer.

25.   *"Stuck-up" Lady*. c. 1910.
Whereabouts unknown

26.   *Bureaucrat*. 1917.
Watercolor, 11¾ x 6¾". Private collection

27.   *Motorists*. 1908.
Ink and watercolor, 11¾ x 7¼". Private collection, Paris

28.   *Grotesque Figure in a Dressing Gown*. 1913.
Watercolor and gouache, 11⅜ x 7½". Private collection

29. *Four Bathers*. c. 1920. Oil, 29½ x 39¼". Private collection, Switzerland

Meanwhile, at a time when he was producing a series of major paintings, Rouault had undertaken a labor which, with its virile black-and-white images, is in a sense a recapitulation of his work. This was the series of etchings, the *Miserere* (see p. 42).

Each plate in this enormous *summa* explores a fundamental theme—Society, Maternity, Labor, Brotherhood, War, Death, Resurrection; each etching achieves a profound, unforeseen, and moving correspondence between a biblical psalm and some aspect of contemporary life. This synthesis of the eternal and the transitory plays a by no means negligible part in the essential value of the *Miserere* series. In these images time seems to have been abolished, yielding to an affirmation of eternity. The two underlying themes of the work, contrition and calamity, are not juxtaposed—they are so closely bound together that one could find no way to separate them.

In the history of printmaking what do we find that is comparable in power to these dark images? We have only the series of etchings in which Rembrandt transposed certain episodes from the life of Christ into the milieu of his own time and Goya's terrifying series on the *Disasters of War*. Rouault began each plate of his *Miserere* anew several

times. Each takes hold of us and leaves us with an unforgettable vision.

Undoubtedly Rouault was thinking of the *Miserere*, whose publication was postponed during World War II, when he again depicted that unrestrained ferocity that makes men wolves to men in his *Homo Homini Lupus* (colorplate 46). In this painting he shows us a hanged man swinging from a gibbet before a village in flames in the distance. Rouault seems to proclaim the man's innocence, giving the whiteness of his shirt the violence of a cry. This use of color to speak directly to our sensibility brings us to a discussion of Rouault's technique.

Rouault was none too fond of explaining his working methods as a creative artist, which he summed up in three words—"form, color, harmony." Yet let us try to understand, with his pictures before us and by referring to the various stages of his career, what sort of brushstrokes he used, what tonalities made up his palette, and how he handled his pigments.

First came that elliptical stroke, sketched in, then affirmed and sustained, that turns back upon itself and, with the force of a whirlwind, hurls the artist's forms into space. At times it broadens, surrounding his main figures with an

30. *Nude*. c. 1925. Oil, 31½ x 23⅝".
Private collection

outline like the lead in the old stained-glass windows that Rouault restored when he worked with Tamoni as an apprentice glass painter.

Like Picasso—and at the same time, around 1905—Rouault had a Blue Period, but his palette can be distinguished from all others by its characteristic blue that chills into green and is then warmed, in the smooth flesh of his young women, into tones bordering on amethyst. Out of economic necessity he worked on paper at that time, using colored inks, which he sometimes mixed with watercolor or gouache, and punctuating his images with a few touches of pastel.

Next came the fluid, volatile textures, created through the use of turpentine washes, of Rouault's clowns and his fairground parades—for example, the *Clown* now at Dumbarton Oaks (colorplate 12). A yellow the color of old copper appears in his *Versailles (The Fountain)* and the brushwork is very free (colorplate 8). Gliding and firm, it is at times calligraphic, sprinkling the canvas with tiny brilliant spots.

Soon after this, the planes acquire greater amplitude; the pigment, now more distinctive than in the oil washes, begins to model the forms, as in *The Bride* and in *The Condemned Man* and *Conjurer* of 1907; it expands and solidifies, becoming richly palpable in *Pierrot (Profile)* and *Old Clown with White Dog* (colorplates 22, 23). Unlike the technique one usually sees in the work of the best painters, who modulate the nuances of their colors carefully, Rouault does not stress color for its own sake. From the beginning his color is at one with his drawing and remains under its domination. Already, however, this color has a life of its own. As pigment it is momentarily thinned to a liquid and then solidified after having been worked, ground, and kneaded (see, for exam-

ple, *The Little Family* of 1932). Soon after, in 1937, comes *The Old King*, a work whose pictorial elements are as forceful as the hieratic profile of its subject (colorplate 29). Here the powerful brilliance of the carmines and blues and the astonishing density of the more subdued colors remind one of Medieval Limoges enamels. Looking at *The Old King*, one can follow the painter's method more clearly than anywhere else. In it he traces and stresses the contours above all, even renewing them if they have been lost beneath the color, which is laid on with broad, consistent touches or, at times, with sweeping brushstrokes.

Toward 1945 Rouault's painting acquires a new serenity and, as in his *Veronica* (colorplate 39), a more communicative religious fervor. Then it becomes even more emphatic, bristling with violent colors as he establishes his forms and cleverly and unobtrusively gives a hierarchic and unified order to the whole, which seems to be composed in planes (*The Flight into Egypt I*; colorplate 40). His light is *invented* and distributed in the service of the picture as a whole. Indeed, is it correct to call it light? Is it not rather, as in the work of El Greco, a glow?

And how should one describe Rouault's landscapes which, when they are not chilled by moonlight, have the colors of ripe fruit—or those autumn pictures in which he depicts the roads that climb Mount Carmel? These are often peopled with figures, one of whom stands out—always the same one, the one in white, the one clothed in the seamless robe.

Soon now the pigment thickens, grows increasingly dense and encrusted. Unequally distributed, it shows swellings, hollow passages, and second thoughts—evidence of a lengthy process of working and reworking. The result suggests some geological cross section of precious substances made accessible to our view.

Next comes the highly colored palette of the painter's last years. In these pictures his touch is felt everywhere and nowhere; the color seems to have been applied with a finger or spread with the palm of the hand within the encircling outlines. Everywhere one senses the presence and the quivering energy of that touch—its communication to and within the material of the painting of something that surpasses and magnifies it. The pigment is worked and kneaded, made to rise like a loaf of bread, tilled like a field marked by the passage of man. In places Rouault leaves a trail of vibrating lapis lazuli, vermilion, or silver-white, so that the subject represented—*Biblical Landscape* (colorplate 47); *The Flight into Egypt II* (colorplate 48); *Sarah*, 1956—appears to melt into a marvelous flow of lava.

In considering Rouault's painting, has enough attention ever been given to the rare and profound originality of the faces in his last paintings—those of the harlequins and Pierrots, the faces and the profiles of the characters he

31. *Workers' Demands (Leftist Neighborhood)*. 1930.
Pastel. Whereabouts unknown

32. *Peasant with White Horse*. c. 1938. Oil, 17⅜ x 13". Private collection, Paris

33.   *Peasant Woman*. 1938. Oil, 41 x 29¼". Formerly collection Ambroise Vollard

34. *Green-nosed Clown*. c. 1926.
Oil, 26 x 19″. Private collection, Japan

35. *Dancer*. 1932. Oil. Private collection

represented from the circus or legends? They are sum-
marized in *The Holy Countenance*, which dominates them
all (colorplate 26). Their bouquets of color are the old
painter's farewell to temporal life, the metamorphosis of his
art into a final salutation and testament.

This was the Rouault I knew. In the apartment near the Gare
de Lyons, where he had his studio, we had enthusiastic
conversations during which the painter interspersed his
monologues with innumerable parenthetical remarks and
incidental thoughts, which he then failed to complete.

I would gaze at his great dolmen-like forehead, while his
ocean-blue eyes rested on me benevolently. The expression
of that broad face was one of concentration, while at the
corners of his mouth there survived a restrained hint of a
bitterness that he had put behind him. He spoke slowly, as

though searching, and then all of a sudden an emphatic
sentence would come out in a rush.

As he talked, Rouault would accompany what he said
with a kind of mime. He would jump up and sit down again,
returning constantly to the three subjects that were his
leitmotivs—his teacher, Gustave Moreau, about whom he
could talk forever; his dealer, Ambroise Vollard, who was
killed in an accident in 1939 and against whose heirs he had
won a lawsuit; and his official and more than slightly grudg-
ing recognition by the Institut. He had recognized that he
could never truly take his place there ever since the day long
ago when his master, who was a member, had wryly re-
marked to him from his sickbed: "I would gladly leave you
my Academician's dress, but you would burst it at the
seams."

With Rouault one never had to break the ice. He accepted everyone at his own level and was always ready to

36.   *The Little Family*. 1932. Oil, 81⅞ x 45⅝″. Private collection, Paris

37. *Head of Christ*, c. 1937. Oil, 26⅜ x 18⅞". Private collection

38. *Christ and Two Figures*. 1937–38. Oil, 41⅜ x 29½". Formerly collection Ambroise Vollard

listen to the humblest and least fortunate person. Yet he never forgot what his art had cost him—though it was true that he was always encouraged by his admirable wife. During the hardest years she gave piano lessons at the Dominican convent at Asnières, and his daughter Isabelle (whom he called his Antigone) took upon herself all the chores that would have eaten into her father's working hours.

One would search in vain in Rouault's work for one of those moments when even the painting of the best artist, fine though it may be, slides into complacency—a prettified portrait, a still life best suited for a dining room, an image characterized by parish sanctimoniousness. From the beginning Rouault kept his art free of the ephemeral fancies of fashion and taste to which his trenchant and aggressive honesty made no concessions. Neither material necessity, nor honors, nor the appeal of the topical could make any inroads into his love of simplicity or touch that childlike soul that he managed to preserve from the least demoralization. To the end he remained what he had always been—the

enemy of complacency and falsehood, a man without vanity. "Like it or not," he wrote to me, "I am just a poor primitive afloat on the bottomless sea of painting."

"But all the same," I shall be told, "your Rouault was not without faults. Have not other painters pushed their researches further than he? Have not some of his contemporaries shown a more delicate sensibility or been greater inventors of forms? And furthermore," the devil's advocate whispers into my ear, "in your Rouault's painting, in spite of its associations with the art of Byzantium and Ravenna (well assimilated, it is true), are there not rather too many Pierrots and Christs turning up on every scrap of canvas, even though they aren't placed against a background of garlands? And besides, what is one to make of his indifference to what was happening during his lifetime? Although he had close relationships with some contemporary authors, philosophers, and geologists (for example, Joris-Karl Huysmans, Léon Bloy, Jacques Maritain, and Pierre Termier), he does not seem to have been affected—nor even so

39. *Spanish Woman*. 1937. Oil, small format.
Formerly collection Ambroise Vollard

40. *Nude*. c. 1939. Oil, 13⅜ x 7⅞".
Georges Rouault Studio

41. *Acrobat*. c. 1939. Oil. Whereabouts unknown

42. *The Bluebird*. 1939.
Oil and gouache, 22⅞ x 16½". Private collection, Paris

much as grazed—by the ideas on art and the experiments in it that tormented the painters who were his rivals—the Symbolists, Nabis, Fauves, or Cubists."

My reply to these reservations, which one sometimes hears formulated, is that an artist can develop not only in agreement with his times, but also in reaction against them. The failure to follow the fluctuations of external events, even if these can be a source of real interest for the arts, does not signify that a man is insensitive to that other reality that lives away from the mainstream in the wild places of the soul.

In February 1946, Rouault wrote to me: "I have the feeling that I am a difficult painter, and, as certain landscape painters of my youth might have put it, 'Perhaps I am not truly immersed in the *atmosphere*—either yesterday or today—of this somewhat legendary art.' Yet I hope all the same [that I am] sensitive enough to human feelings, although masculine and severe, even bitter. When I tried twice for the Prix de Rome, I was *already in spirit* inclined toward this art."

Yes, Rouault was never, as they say, "in the mainstream,"

and this is certainly the secret of the timelessness of his art. He did not paint in the style of his times. Furthermore, his plasticity, his color, and his conceptions are not related to any school of painting that could be dated without hesitation. Indeed, setting aside the dimensions and genre of his pictures, as well as the chemistry of his pigments, we would not be especially surprised to learn that his work came to us from the high point of the Middle Ages. The people in his paintings do not wear the costumes of a particular period; their dress is timeless, their expression is the universal expression of mankind.

As for the large number of scenes from the Gospels that he painted after a certain period of his life, to reproach him with these would make no more sense than to do the same to Giotto, El Greco, or Rembrandt. Rouault did not treat sacred art as something separate. "There is no such thing as sacred art," he used to tell me. "There is simply art, and that is enough to fill a lifetime." Surely the essential thing is that his painting touches and moves us, always retaining its disturbing quality. What is most important is that, in his difficult search for the figure of

43. *Christian Spirit (Christ in the House of Martha and Mary)*. c. 1945. Oil, 18⅛ x 25⅝". Private collection, Paris

44. *The Holy Countenance*. c. 1946. Oil, 19⅝ x 14⅛". Private collection, Paris

Christ, this painter, with his vision of the Savior and of the Holy Countenance, succeeded in taking his place beside the creators of the most moving images of the past.

More than anyone else—more than Picasso, whose Italianisms are frequent; more than Matisse, who hoped to find an absolute in art itself—Rouault decisively separated himself from Renaissance humanism in order to join the company of those who worked on the cathedrals. As their successor, he "dreamed of working anonymously," for to him spiritual man was more complete than materialistic man, and the saint more complete than the fine athlete or even the great thinker. "I have made a clean sweep of the beauties of paradise," he used to say with a smile.

From the beginning of his career Rouault had a limited choice of directions before him. He could either pursue routine art in the facile tradition of the École or, under the influence of the fashion of the day, return to some form of primitive adamitism—or, again, he could turn his efforts toward an artificial manner of painting that would end in a dry emptiness.

Rouault had no need to hesitate among these possibilities, each one as pernicious as the other. His strong personality, his inner equilibrium, his disgust with the idea of fabricating an aesthetic doctrine for himself led him simply to follow his natural inclinations. They caused him to listen to his creative intuition, which goes beyond common sense and beyond the limits of deductive intelligence, taking a path that runs paral-

45. *Dancers*. c. 1948.
Oil, 16½ x 13".
Private collection

46. *In the Moonlight*. c. 1948. Oil.
Collection Ahrenberg, Stockholm

47. *The Sibyl of Cumae*. 1947.
Oil, 24⅜ x 14⅝".
Private collection, Paris

lel to, yet is less obvious than, that indicated by a logically determined perspective.

Guided by the inner light to which his art of darkness and humanity guides us, Rouault went through the stages of his development with the avid strength of the visionary. From his prostitutes to the circus and courtroom scenes, from *Versailles (The Fountain)* (colorplate 8) to the final landscapes, from his *Nativity* to his *Holy Countenance*, his art—proof against all wavering of purpose—constantly maintained its high level, renewing itself without ever lapsing into the slightest mannerisms.

As a result, Georges Rouault has emerged as one of those who carry the most weight in the field of pictorial expression during the first half of the twentieth century, rich though it has been in artistic production. The further we move away from the years that were his years of fulfillment, the more he seems to grow, man and painter united in an inseparable whole.

48. *Carmencita*. 1947. Oil, 19¼ x 12¼". Private collection, Milan

49. *Ecce Homo*. 1952.
Oil, 19⅝ x 17¾″.
Private collection, Paris

50. *Winter*. c. 1946.
Oil and gouache, 15¾ x 12¼″.
Private collection

51. Study for frontispiece of *Les Fleurs du Mal*. 1945. Oil, 9⅞ x 7⅞″.
Formerly collection Ambroise Vollard

52. *Winter*. 1946. Oil, 10⅝ x 10⅝". Private collection, France

53.   *Portrait of Baudelaire*. 1926. Lithograph, 8¼ x 6¼″. From *Souvenirs intimes*

GRAPHIC WORKS

54. *The Flood*. 1910. Watercolor, 9½ x 12¼″. Private collection, Paris

If an artistic medium exists in which certain similarities more or less unite the most diverse artists, it is that of the print. The reason, no doubt, is that in printmaking the painter or sculptor must submit to the requirements of what seems to be a manual craft, a technique with which professional illustrators often remain content, hardly bothering to move beyond it.

In spite of this partial limitation inherent in the medium, Rouault stands out as a lithographer and etcher, as he does in his painting, by virtue of a character unique to himself. Let us attempt to summarize Rouault's activities in this field while we await publication of the catalogue of his engraved work now being prepared by his daughter Isabelle and his grandson Olivier Nouaille in collaboration with Jacques Guignard.

In the beginning Rouault alternated between etchings and lithographs. His *Baudelaire* served as the frontispiece to the second edition of his *Souvenirs intimes;* the first edition, which had appeared in 1926, had contained six lithographs. Rouault's portrait is a perfect evocation of the "sharp point of a somewhat lofty soul"—which is how Rouault saw the author of *Les Fleurs du Mal*.

Next came the series of lithographs made for Frapier in which Rouault poured out his caustic, ironic humor, showing us the demagogue with his raised fist, the confrontation of the augurs, the parade of the fairground performers, the poses of dancers and clowns. The six lithographs of his *Paysages légendaires* (1929) have a more ornamental quality. Heavily inked, rather mysterious, they are a prelude to the Gospel scenes that he would develop later.

In his *Petite Banlieue (Depressed Suburbs)* of 1929, a series of six lithographs, Rouault recounts in images his most searing childhood memories of Belleville. In one print, for example, a hearse advances slowly toward a wall beyond which crosses and cypresses appear.

Following this, in the twenty-two copperplates for Vollard's mediocre book, *Les Réincarnations du Père Ubu* (1932), Rouault was initiated into the technique of etching. He was to practice this medium again and soon followed up these prints with new experiments involving color, the result being his *Le Cirque de l'étoile filante* (1938) and his *Passion* (1939).

In his prints of this period Rouault developed a whole "cuisine"—an elaborate blend of techniques—never confining himself to the traditional methods that had been used ever since engraving on metal was invented by the Italian goldsmith Maso Finiguerra in the middle of the fifteenth century. In this type of work, as in his painting, Rouault always valued sensibility and expressiveness above technical knowledge and virtuosity.

During World War I, when his mastery of his technique as an etcher was already complete, Rouault began work on the black-and-white plates of the work that is incontestably the chief creation of contemporary printmaking, his *Miserere*. This collection of fifty-eight etchings, executed with complete freedom, was accompanied by texts written by the artist. Ambroise Vollard had the flair to have this monumental folio printed, but the plates, which emerged from the press in 1927, were not gathered into a bound volume until 1948, nine years after Vollard's death.

I recall being present in 1948 when the book was first shown to the public at the gallery of Odette des Garets, where it was exhibited along with the painter's latest pictures. Only 450 copies of the *Miserere* were printed, rather than the 500 that had been planned, because the war and other circumstances had caused the loss of, or damage to, a certain number of proofs. The work as a whole is a summary of almost all of Rouault's major themes. Each plate, originally executed as a drawing in Chinese ink, was later rendered as a painting. "Starting from there," Rouault said, "I tried—and with what difficulty—to preserve the original rhythm and design. I worked on each plate with different tools, with more or less happy results. There is nothing secret there. Dissatisfied, I went over each subject again and again, making as many as twelve or fifteen successive states."[7]

After the work was completed, the copperplates were scored, as is the custom, and Rouault rejected the proposal, made by a senior diplomat living in Paris, that some of them be coated with gold and set into the walls of the United States Embassy.

7. Georges Rouault, Preface to *Miserere*, Paris, 1948.

Rouault's *Miserere* is an inner world peopled with deeply moving figures whose accentuated outlines, often consisting of double lines, enlarge them. In every part of this world one feels the presence of the war—and indeed Rouault at one time thought of adding this title to that of *Miserere*. Each plate is either an affirmation of the individual and of humanity or a condemnation of those who think themselves entitled to rule over others. The artist has given his own features to the sad effigy of the clown. In some places we see remembered scenes of the decayed suburb with its curtainless houses, its people who pursue "the hard trade of living," the mother bent over her child, the lady from the grand part of town who thinks she possesses a reserved ticket to heaven. In others it is the condemned man that he depicts, the cold teeth of winter that bite the poor, the ruin made by the war that is always believed to be the last, the burned countryside, the wounded borne up by angels—death, the Resurrection.

As we have seen, Rouault's work as a printmaker began with an image of Baudelaire, and it was with Baudelaire and the fourteen plates made during his life and inspired by *Les Fleurs du Mal* that the publication of his prints was to end. These

Rouault attached great importance to the *Miserere* series. He was happy, as he said, to see its publication "before disappearing from this planet,"[8] and in order to give everyone access to the compositions that make up this great book, he had them reproduced in a small format—"In a form," as Maurice Morel said, " that would enable people other than millionaires to contemplate its images and meditate on them at leisure."

The hand has achieved such mastery of the tool that the etchings of this series seem to have been painted. Etcher's needle, brush, acid, roulette—every tool was useful to this man who said, "Someone hands me a copperplate . . . and I go at it."[9]

8. Georges Rouault, Preface to *Miserere*, New York, 1952.
9. Ambroise Vollard, *Souvenirs d'un marchand de tableaux*, Paris, 1927.

55. *Worker*. 1914.
Probably from André Suarès's *Passion*

56. *The Three Crosses*. 1929. Lithograph. From *Paysages légendaires*

57. *Untitled*. 1929. Lithograph. From *Paysages légendaires*

58. *Untitled*. c. 1929. Lithograph. From *Paysages légendaires*

59. *Tête-à-tête (Confidences)*. 1925–27. Lithograph, 11¼ x 9¼".
Éditions Frapier

etchings, which were published in 1960 through the efforts of his daughters after Rouault's death, were shown at the Galerie Creuzevault.

The genesis of this work can be placed in 1918 when Rouault informed Vollard of his desire to do a "Baudelaire" under the title *Danse macabre ou Les Fleurs du Mal*. In 1925 he etched the compositions for this work. Ambroise Vollard had 500 copies of the plates printed separately by Jacquemin, but did not publish them in book form. Because some of the sheets went astray, the publication, strictly speaking, contains only 450 plates. Jacques Guignard reminds us that a "series of twenty-six Chinese-ink wash drawings, in a much smaller format than that of the black-and-white etchings, is in some cases closely related with the unfinished plates, in others with the definitive ones." Isabelle Rouault and Geneviève Nouaille state: "Our father later undertook the illustration of the same work in color" (of these prints, twelve unfinished plates are known), but in 1939 this work was interrupted by the accidental death of Vollard.

Rouault believed that a poem should not be illustrated too precisely. He knew that the best procedure for the artist was to transpose it into images, showing its visual repercussions on an artist who has entered into the atmosphere of the text "like a modest and understanding brother."

I know of no image so striking as the *Danse macabre* of that female skeleton who rises between two shutters "with her lipless and gumless smile, and her gaze that is only a hole filled with shadow...," a dismal apparition of death "whose head, dissected by time, rises coquettishly from its bodice as a parched bouquet rises from its screw of paper."[10]

These etchings by Rouault are surely as tragic, as penetrating, and as unforgettable as the poems that inspired them, poems that were present in the painter's mind throughout most of his life, so that he also based several oil paintings on them, as well as a series of gouaches that bear the title *Fleurs du Mal*.

10. Charles Baudelaire, *Salon de 1859, La Sculpture* in *Curiosités esthétiques*, Paris, 1928, p. 354. Baudelaire was inspired to make these comments by a sculpture by Jules Christophe that the poet was sorry not to see exhibited at the Salon of 1859.

60. *Juggler*. 1925–27.
Lithograph, 12¼ x 8¼".
Éditions Frapier

61. *Buffoon*. 1926.
Lithograph, 13⅜ x 8⅝".
Éditions Frapier

62.   *Depressed Suburbs*. 1929. Lithograph, 12⅝ x 8⅝". Éditions des Quatre Chemins

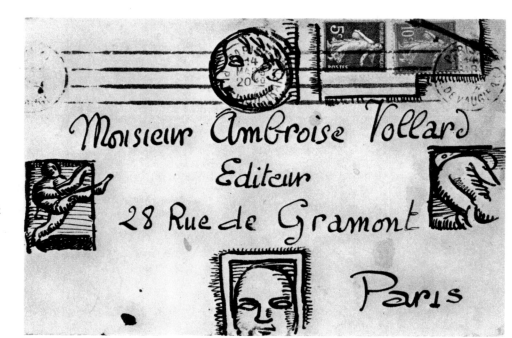

63.   Envelope with drawings by Rouault

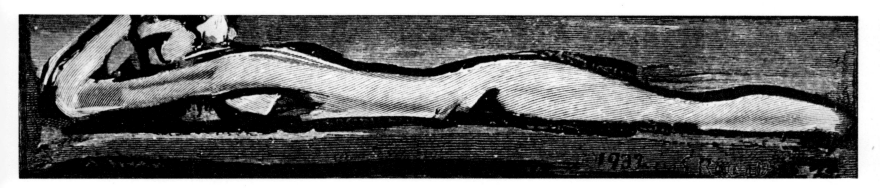

64.   *Nude*. 1928. Wood engraving. From *Le Cirque de l'étoile filante*

65. *The Freed Slave*. 1928. Etching, 8½ x 11¾″. From *Les Réincarnations du Père Ubu*

66. *Blacks*. Etching. From *Les Réincarnations du Père Ubu*

67. *This Will Be the Last, Little Father*. 1927. Etching, 16½ x 23⅝″. From *Miserere*

68.   *My Sweet Country, Where Are You?* 1927. Etching, 16½ x 23⅝". From *Miserere*

69.   *The Difficult Profession of Living.* 1922.
Etching, 18⅞ x 14⅛".
From *Miserere*

70. *It Would Be So Good to Love*. 1923.
Etching, 22¾ x 16¼".
From *Miserere*

71. *The Street of the Lonely Ones*. 1927. Etching, 16½ x 23⅝". From *Miserere*

72.   *Don't We All Wear Makeup?* 1927. Etching, 22¼ x 16¾". From *Miserere*

73. *When You Fall Asleep My Pretty One*. 1927.
Etching, 10⅝ x 14⅛".
From *Les Fleurs du Mal*

74. *Danse Macabre*. 1927.
Etching, 14⅛ x 10¼".
From *Les Fleurs du Mal*

75. *Debauchery and Death Are Two Nice Girls*. 1926. Etching, 12½ x 9¾″. From *Les Fleurs du Mal*

76. *Self-Portrait*. 1926. Lithograph, 9 x 6¾". Frontispiece from *Souvenirs intimes*

77.   *Portrait of Joris-Karl Huysmans*. 1926.
Lithograph, 9 x 6¾".
From *Souvenirs intimes*

79.   *Portrait of Léon Bloy*. 1926.
Lithograph, 9½ x 6½".
From *Souvenirs intimes*

78.   *Portrait of Gustave Moreau*. 1926.
Lithograph, 9 x 6¾".
From *Souvenirs intimes*

80. Photograph of Rouault
while a pupil of Gustave Moreau

81. Rouault with his wife
and their children, Isabelle, Michel, and Geneviève, in 1915

82. Georges and Isabelle Rouault, 1952

83–84. Rouault at work in his studio, July 1953

BIOGRAPHICAL OUTLINE

1871   May 27, Georges Henri Rouault is born in Paris in a cellar (51 rue de la Villette, Belleville) during a bombardment of the northern section of the capital by the troops of the "Versailles government." Paris itself is in the hands of the Commune. His father, Alexandre Rouault, from Montfort in Brittany, is thirty-one and a cabinetmaker by trade. His mother, Marie-Louise Alexandrine Champdavoine, born in Paris, is twenty-seven.

1881   Pays frequent visits to his aunts, who live in the rue de Sévigné with their father, Alexandre Champdavoine. The latter—an ardent admirer of Rembrandt, Corot, Daumier, Courbet, and Manet—gives his grandson his first instruction in art.

1885–90   Serves his apprenticeship as a stained-glass painter, first with Tamoni, then with Hirsch. Works on the restoration of windows and attends evening classes at the École des Arts Décoratifs in the rue de l'École de Médecine. The French painter Albert Besnard asks him to execute the stained-glass windows for the École de Pharmacie from his cartoons, but Rouault declines the offer out of loyalty to Hirsch. Reads and is strongly influenced by Léon Bloy's *La Femme pauvre*. Decides that he will become a painter, and on December 3, 1890, enters the École des Beaux-Arts in the studio of Elie Delaunay.

1891–92   Delaunay dies on September 5, 1891, and is succeeded by Gustave Moreau. Rouault becomes Moreau's favorite pupil. Among his fellow students are Matisse, Marquet, Lehmann, Evenepoel, and Manguin. Paints a series of religious subjects in a Rembrandtesque style.

1893   March 31, Moreau insists that he compete for the Prix de Rome; the subject is The Ordeal of Samson. Rouault fails to win the prize, which is awarded to a man named Mitricey.

1894   February 6, is awarded second prize in the Fortin d'Ivry competition for his painting *Coriolanus in the House of Tullius*. In July, wins the Chénavard prize for *The Child Jesus Among the Doctors*.

1895   Competes a second time for the Prix de Rome; the subject is The Dead Christ Mourned by the Holy Women. Once again he fails to win, and the prize is awarded to an inferior painter, a pupil of Bonnat named Larée.

1896   Exhibits his entry for the Prix de Rome at the Salon des Artistes Français.

1897   Is represented at the Salon de la Rose-Croix by a drawing, *The Dead Christ*. Sends several landscapes and the *Bathers* to the Salon of this year.

1898   April 18, Gustave Moreau dies of cancer at the age of seventy-two; Rouault is profoundly affected by the loss of his teacher. Moreau bequeaths his studio and collections to the government on the condition that they be transformed into a museum bearing his name.

1901   Paints romantic landscapes, religious compositions, and Paris scenes. At the end of the year, makes a retreat to a Benedictine abbey at Ligugé, near Poitiers, where Joris-Karl Huysmans is trying to organize a brotherhood of artists.

1903   January 14, the Musée Gustave Moreau, rue de La Rochefoucauld, Paris, is inaugurated, and Rouault is appointed curator. Participates in the founding of the Salon d'Automne with Desvallières, Matisse, Marquet, Piot, and the critic Y. Rambosson. Is represented by two paintings in the first exhibition.

1904   March, meets Léon Bloy, who eventually becomes a close friend. At the Salon d'Automne, exhibits a large number of watercolors and drawings in the dark tones of his strongly original new manner; his subjects are prostitutes, clowns, acrobats, and landscapes. The public sneers at these "gloomy" paintings.

1905   Exhibits a triptych entitled *Prostitutes* at the Salon d'Automne. One of the panels represents M. and Mme. Poulot, characters from Léon Bloy's novel *La Femme pauvre*; the other two panels show a prostitute and Terpsichore. In the "Cage aux Fauves" at the same Salon, exhibits pictures of street and circus performers and clowns.

1906   February, exhibition of Rouault's work is held at the Berthe Weil Gallery. Later in the year, he shows at the Salon d'Automne.

1907   Meets Ambroise Vollard through Rouault's ceramist, Metthey. Paints *Condemned Man*, the first in his series of courtroom scenes inspired by the people at the Tribunal de la Seine, which he attends for nearly a year with his friend Deputy Prosecutor Granier.

1908   January 27, marries Marthe Le Sidaner, by whom he will have four children: Geneviève, Isabelle, Michel, and Agnès. Continues work on his courtroom series; also paints poor people, peasants, and workers.

1910   February 24–March 5, has first one-man show at the Galerie Druet, 10 rue Royale, Paris. On April 14, an article about his work by Jacques Rivière appears in the *Nouvelle Revue Française*.

1911   Begins his friendship with André Suarès. On December 11, his second one-man show opens at the Galerie Druet; on December 15, enthusiastic article by Louis Vauxcelles appears in *Gil Blas*.

1912 Moves to Versailles, 36 rue de l'Orangerie. Jacques and Raïssa Maritain, to whom he was introduced by Léon Bloy, are his neighbors. (Some authorities date this move to 1911.)

1917 Vollard becomes Rouault's dealer. Later, Vollard gives the artist a studio on the first floor of his own house, 28 rue Martignac, Paris, enabling the painter to complete several hundred canvases. Vollard commissions Rouault to illustrate *Les Réincarnations du Père Ubu;* work on this project continues for ten years. In agreement with Vollard, Rouault begins the *Miserere* and *Les Fleurs du Mal;* these works absorb much of the artist's time for some years.

1918 Abandons watercolor and gouache to work in oil. Paints religious subjects, especially Christ's Passion. His palette becomes more colorful.

1919 October 17, *The Child Jesus Among the Doctors*, which was bought by the government in 1917, is placed in the museum at Colmar. It is the first painting by Rouault to be exhibited in a museum.

1920 One-man show at the Galerie La Licorne is organized by Dr. D. Girardin, one of his principal collectors. Among his other collectors are M. and Mme. Marcel Sembat, Mme. Olivier Saincère, Stéphane Piot, Gustave Coquiot, Baignères, Dutilleul, Leclanché, John Quinn, M. and Mme. Henri Simon, Mme. Heddy Hahnloser, and Mme. Louise Hervieu.

1921 First monograph on Rouault, written by Michel Puy, appears in the collection *Les Peintres français nouveaux*.

1922 One-man show at the Galerie Barbazanges.

1924 April 22–May 2, large retrospective exhibition is held at the Galerie Druet. On May 15, Jacques Maritain publishes an important essay on Rouault in *La Revue Universelle*.

1926 Publishes *Souvenirs intimes*, which is illustrated with lithographs. Book by Georges Charensol containing thirty-nine reproductions of works by Rouault is published.

1929 Creates settings and costumes for Diaghilev's ballet *The Prodigal Son;* the score is by Prokofiev and the choreography by Balanchine. The ballet is performed at the Sarah Bernhardt Theater on May 21, 29, 31, and June 4, 6, 12. Toward the end of the year, visits Montana-sur-Sierre in the Valais, Switzerland. His clothes catch fire while he is dressed as Santa Claus to entertain the children and his hands are severely burned.

1930 The Under Secretary of State for the Fine Arts refuses to acquire a painting by Rouault for the Musée du Luxembourg that was recommended by the museum's acquisitions committee. Begins a series of color etchings for *Cirque de l'étoile filante*, for which he wrote the text, and for André Suarès's *Passion*. First exhibitions outside France: St. George Gallery, London; J.B. Neumann Gallery, Munich; Brummer Gallery, New York; and The Arts Club, Chicago.

1932 Paints *The Injured Clown* and *The Little Family*, which Mme. Cuttoli has reproduced as a tapestry by the Aubusson craftsmen. Mrs. Chester Dale gives the Musée du Luxembourg a canvas by Rouault, his first in that museum.

1937 June–October, retrospective exhibition of forty-two canvases is held in a special room at the Petit Palais. On seeing this important collection, Lionello Venturi decides to write a monograph on Rouault (it is published in New York in 1940).

1938 Exhibition of Rouault's graphic work at the Museum of Modern Art, New York.

1939 Ambroise Vollard dies on July 22, shortly before the outbreak of World War II.

1940–41 Exhibitions in Boston, Washington, and San Francisco.

1943 Publication of *Divertissement*.

1945 Retrospective exhibition of 161 works is held at the Museum of Modern Art, New York. Designs five windows for church at Plateau d'Assy, France.

1946 Braque-Rouault exhibition is held in April at the Tate Gallery, London.

1947 March 19, wins his case against Vollard's heirs when the court rules that a painter remains owner of his work until he has unconditionally handed it over to another person and orders that all Rouault's unfinished canvases must be returned to him (119 of these are never returned, however). *Stella Vespertina* is published by René Drouin. Exhibition of forty paintings at the gallery of Odette des Garets in the rue de Courcelles.

1948 April–June, retrospective exhibition of 166 works at the Kunsthaus, Zurich. Visits Switzerland and, for the first time, Italy. France sends twenty-five paintings and twelve etchings by Rouault to the Venice Biennale. On November 5, in the presence of a court official, burns 315 canvases from among those returned to him by court order. From November 27–December 21, the *Miserere* is presented at the gallery of Odette des Garets.

1949 Executes first maquettes for the enamels made in the workshop of the abbey at Ligugé. Visits Belgium and Holland.

1951 June 6, the Centre Catholique des Intellectuels Français organizes "Hommage à Rouault" at the Palais de Chaillot to celebrate the artist's eightieth birthday. That evening Abbé Morel's film on the *Miserere* is shown to the public for the first time. Is made a Commander of the Legion of Honor.

1952 Retrospective exhibitions at the Palais des Beaux-Arts, Brussels; the Stedelijk Museum, Amsterdam; and the Musée National d'Art Moderne, Paris.

1953 Retrospective exhibitions at the Cleveland Museum of Art, the Museum of Modern Art in New York, the Los Angeles County Museum of Art, the National Museum of Art in Tokyo, and the Osaka Municipal Museum of Art.

1956 Exhibition at Albi in the Musée Toulouse-Lautrec (Palais de la Berbie).

1958 February 13, dies in Paris at the age of eighty-seven. The government gives him a state funeral. On February 17, a short speech is made by Abbé Maurice Morel during the ceremony at the church of St. Germain-des-Prés. M. Billières, Minister of Public Education, gives a eulogy of the painter in the square in front of the church and a message from André Lhote is read in the name of French artists.

COLORPLATES

Colorplate 2

THE ORDEAL OF SAMSON
1893
Oil on canvas, 57½ x 44⅞"
Collection Mr. and Mrs. George Gard de Sylva

In 1892 Rouault tested his skill by painting a *Job and His Friends,* the subject set that year for the Prix de Rome (the prize was awarded to a man named Lavergne). The following year Rouault was officially invited to enter the competition, but his painting was not awarded the prize. This was given instead to a certain M. Mitricey for a weak profile of Samson, painted in the Grand Guignol style, and to a M. Trigoulet for a picture, only slightly better, in which Samson is seen full face, tugging at the handgrips of a huge stone wheel.

Rouault had painted this far more moving interpretation of the subject. In his work we see Samson surrounded by his torturers who, having put out Samson's eyes, are now beating him before a mob of shouting, contemptuous Philistines.

Gustave Moreau was disappointed that his favorite pupil was passed over; to encourage him and to show Rouault the value that he attached to the painting, Moreau himself made a sketch of it.

In Rouault's *Samson* there is already evidence of his need to render his subject with an expressiveness that is completely free of theatricality. Two years later— again to his master's great disappointment—Rouault failed a second time to win the Prix de Rome, which went to a melodramatic picture by a pupil of Bonnat named Larée. The subject that year was *The Dead Christ Mourned by the Holy Women.*

As always, success went to the mediocre. "How many of those clever and diligent pupils I saw at the studio," Rouault used to say. "In front of the model they would begin with the hair on the top of the head, and at the end of the week, or even before, the good men had finished, down to the last reflections on the toenails."

Colorplate 3

NIGHT LANDSCAPE (THE WORKYARD)
1897
Watercolor and pastel, 25⅝ x 33½"
Collection Mme. Henri Simon, Paris

It is common for an artist, guided by his creative intuition, to produce a major work at the beginning of his career. This was the case with Rouault in this nocturnal landscape. With its allusions to working-class life and its image of ceaseless conflict, this watercolor, which Rouault heightened with pastel, seems a prophetic work. Painted while the artist was still a pupil of Gustave Moreau at the École des Beaux-Arts in Paris, it foreshadowed his future achievement.

In this painting one sees Rouault moving into that world of dark tonalities that can be used effectively only by the most powerful artists, for nothing is more difficult to control than that sombre palette. It must touch the essential if it is to succeed.

What was the atmosphere like in Paris in 1897, the year in which Joris-Karl Huysmans published his novel *La Cathédrale*? Following a demonstration against the admission of women to the school, the École des Beaux-Arts closed its doors for a month. It was the era of the anarchists and of insistent demands made by members of the working class. Isabelle Rouault remembers that her father spoke to her of a gruesome fight among butchers in connection with this *Night Landscape*. It is possible that an episode from this event is depicted in the group of figures on the left, while in the middle ground we have a glimpse of an uprising. In the distance two large, unfinished towers shoot upward among the terraces of a town upon which a shower of rain falls.

Colorplate 4

PROSTITUTES
1903
Oil on canvas, 9⅝ x 9"
Private collection, Bern

This is one of the finest bouquets of color to emerge from Rouault's early palette. Starting with a sordid subject, he has managed to transform it into a delight for our eyes.

Five years after Gustave Moreau's death the mastery of his favorite pupil is already evident in this small picture, which is composed of patches of color and slashing, assertive brushstrokes. The color is so enchanting that it reveals the renunciation that characterizes Rouault's later work, that is, his decision not to follow the path—I will not say of facility, but of simple charm and seductiveness.

Note the skill with which, by means of free, brilliant, and decisive touches, Rouault achieves the marvelous color harmonies that distinguish his treatment of his subject. These tourmaline blues, vermilions, and resonant blacks, punctuated with white, gray, and pink, cannot help but captivate us.

Rouault was soon to prefer something very different from these attractive tonalities, launching himself into an exploration of the dark and painful depths of the human mystery. Soon he would replace this colorful lyricism with a profound analysis of the human heart and soul. After this his hand would trace such seductive colors only at rare intervals—for example, in *The Equestrienne; The Bluebird;* and *Pierrot as Aristocrat* (colorplate 35). In the future his prostitutes would be marked instead with the tragic seal of human decadence. Thus when he returned to this theme in his *Trio* of 1906, he would give his prostitutes the quality of depravity.

Colorplate 5

BATHERS
1903
Watercolor, 17⅜ x 13"
Private collection, Paris

In 1903 Rouault painted not only prostitutes but also bathing girls. The latter gave him the pretext for a complementary study of the female nude; for while his prostitutes stifle in the tainted air of their rooms, his bathing girls, seated out-of-doors before backgrounds of sky and huge August clouds, are integrated with the landscape. They are made part of it through their poses, reminding us of Cézanne's desire "to unite the curves of women with the shoulders of hills."

At this time Rouault took pleasure in contrasting the firm flesh of these bodies in the open air with the flaccid and swollen flesh of his prostitutes. In this watercolor it is the expression of the free and healthy natural life that gains the upper hand. Poses and gestures are sober. Serenity is in the air. The attitudes of the girls have that grave expressiveness that one sees in some of the pictures of Cézanne, who, as Rouault later wrote in his *Souvenirs intimes*, "remains a difficult painter, far removed from the jugglers and virtuosos."

The chief excellence here is in the suppleness of the brushwork, which obeys an inner rhythm. The picture fans out from the gaze of the two bathing girls, coming toward us from a distant point in space.

Colorplate 6

HEAD OF A TRAGIC CLOWN
1904
Watercolor and pastel, 14⅝ x 10½"
Kunsthaus, Zurich. Bangerter Collection

Among the many pictorial representations of the clown—that figure in English farce so well understood by Shakespeare—I know none as striking, as moving, or as dark as this clown by Rouault. Here the man whose profession it is to make others laugh emerges from the night in which he has stifled his own misery and suffering. He comes out of the darkness like those figures that we see looming up out of the shadows in works by Rembrandt.

Gazing at us from the depths of obscurity, he is a heartbreaking apparition. The whole man is summed up in the face, lacerated by life, scourged by violence, darkened by the effects of our excesses. He has the straightforward and yet defeated look of one who has been smothered by the infiniteness of human weakness. But he knows this. He is aware, and this is what makes him appear to be a living protest against the inequality that prevails among men.

To dare to begin a career with work containing so little appeal for those who seek in art only a charm that will distract them from the monotony of their lives was surely a sign of uncommon strength of character. None of Rouault's contemporaries, not even Bonnard or Matisse, dared to make his debut in this way, in the night. None of them risked so intimidating an art. When one looks at this figure, emerging from so dark a palette, it is easy to understand how an official painter at the Institut of that time, a mediocre man now justly forgotten, could derisively strike a match in front of Rouault's dark paintings at the Salon des Indépendants. He could not have suspected that this "obscurant" would illuminate the future.

Colorplate 7

PITCH-BALL PUPPETS
(THE WEDDING OF NINI-PATTE-EN-L'AIR)
1905
Watercolor, 20½ x 26⅜"
Private collection, Paris

Rouault was always interested in the fairground entertainments that, until quite recently, filled certain quarters of Paris. He was attracted by the strange games, such as the one that consisted of making puppets tip over by throwing large balls stuffed with heavy, spongy material at their heads. This "game of slaughter" *(jeu de massacre)*, which in some regions was also called "The Wedding of Thomas," always centered on a bride. In this picture we see the barker leaning on her elbow, facing the box of balls, about to speak to a young soldier on leave or to some other person tempted to have a try at the "game of slaughter" with a few balls at one *sou* apiece.

The subject was well suited to the experiments with expressiveness that preoccupied Rouault at this time. Drawing with large slashing strokes, he contrived to give his puppets highly individualized faces that express his sense of irony. But the most disquieting figure, which one notices only gradually, is that of the barker, the dreadful woman with her unprepossessing chignon, a drunkard out of one of Bloy's novels. More phantom-like than her puppets, she waits for the gull who will try his skill at her stall.

This watercolor looks as if it were painted with the dregs of some coarse red wine; it exhibits the bare, unadorned drawing of Rouault's first period. His stroke seems to hesitate. It moves around and over the form almost as if it would cross it out. Elliptical, in some places acerbic, Rouault's line has the spontaneity of improvisation.

Two years after this depiction of the whole scene Rouault was to paint an analogous one, a close-up in oil on mounted paper called *Pitch-Ball Puppets* or *The Bride,* that is now in the Tate Gallery.

Colorplate 8

VERSAILLES (THE FOUNTAIN)
1905
Watercolor and pastel, 26⅜ x 20⅞"
Private collection, France

Before moving there in 1912, Rouault sometimes visited Versailles to make studies. The place acted to some extent as a counterbalance to the attention he was giving to working-class life and that of the underworld. He saw in the palace and the pathways of Le Nôtre the realization of work that had been supervised by a single artist. In this highly personal picture he shows us the plume of water spurting up from the great basin of Neptune in front of the long perspective of trees leading to the palace, as well as several promenaders among the trees.

The fountain rises against a sky that is partly blue, partly orange, and the basin that catches the falling water is surrounded by strollers. But the remarkable quality about this inimitable work is its apparent spontaneity. With swift, jaunty touches of the point of the brush—among which the patches of red and blue are brought off, as it were, with a swagger—the painter has created for himself a calligraphy that is full of vivacity. This wonderful assemblage of water, garden, and sky makes clear to us how completely Rouault had freed himself of all the conventions of the École. Each plane, with its slashed accents, carries us into that world of sulphur and fire that this artist miraculously evoked with watercolor and a few strokes of pastel.

Colorplate 9

PROSTITUTE AT HER MIRROR
1906
Watercolor, 28⅜ x 21⅝"
Musée National d'Art Moderne, Paris

Suddenly confronted with harsh reality after the death of Gustave Moreau, his master and protector, Rouault gave what he used to call *le coup de barre* to the course he had temporarily adopted at the École—that is, he radically changed the direction of his work. His *Night Landscape (The Workyard)* (colorplate 3) had been a preparation for this change.

Determined to work with the passionate frankness that we saw in *Versailles (The Fountain)* (colorplate 8), Rouault in *Prostitute at Her Mirror* again took up the theme that was to obsess him for several years. He treated the theme of the prostitute, along with that of the charlatans and courtrooms, as a means of protest against the warts and blemishes of society.

The *Prostitute at Her Mirror* is in no way a descendant of Gustave Moreau's princess-like hetaerae. She gazes at her face in the mirror with a frightening gravity. It is a face whose sadness pierces our hearts.

Here again it is difficult to believe that this dense, terrifying, unforgettable work, which seems to have been made with human flesh and blood, is painted only in watercolor. The public gave a less than friendly reception to this extraordinary picture. But true lovers of art are rare. Most of those who look at paintings do so out of curiosity. They are people who, as Rouault said, "do not enjoy your *present* effort. They demand of you a *past* effort that, in fact, they despised when you were grinding away at the millstone."

Colorplate 10

PARADE

1906
Watercolor and pastel, 18½ x 23⅝"
Private collection, Paris

Rouault's technique at this time was often quite mixed and is sometimes difficult to identify. I have at times hesitated to say what materials were then used by the artist.

We have here a watercolor that has been heightened with pastel. Supreme skill is required to achieve this fluidity and this freedom of brushstroke, this background wash and this sometimes emphatic, sometimes elusive calligraphy. Indeed, it is necessary to have gone beyond technical skill in order to produce such effects of light as, for example, the rare transparency and brightness of the glow that falls upon the clown at the left. With its elliptical line made up of broad and narrow strokes, the almost calligraphic drawing suggests movement itself.

Artists today strive to achieve the refinements of brushstroke at which the Chinese excel. In this *Parade* of 1906 one can already see the whole range of gestures that Rouault had at his disposal, allowing him to move easily from a stroke that scarcely touched the surface to a thick and emphatic outline. The accents here make one think of the agitations of a seismograph or, even more, of those of a cardiogram. Nothing in this painting is derived from a work of the past; it is truly invented. This *Parade* in blue, green, and red appears to be a kind of dialogue, transposed into strokes and colors, while a clown and a dancer emerge in the background.

Colorplate 11

PROSTITUTE

1906

Gouache, watercolor, and pastel, 28 x 21⅝"
Musée d'Art Moderne de la Ville de Paris

Some of Rouault's "girls" make one think of François Villon's Grosse Margot, who was "more swollen than a slimy snail." The example we see here—monumental, tidying her hair as she sits on the sofa—has the force of an archetype; she inscribes herself forever in our memory. This is the Prostitute, the woman who lives with her flesh and by her flesh, pushing away the thought that a time will come when it will yellow and wither.

Of all the girls painted by Rouault, this is the most realistic. And yet she is not made to appear perverted in the manner of those "ladies" Toulouse-Lautrec has shown us in the salons of the rue des Moulins. Nor is she, like Degas's women, caught in a humiliating posture. She is there—inscribed, sculptural, at one and the same time a Pigalle girl and the whore of the Apocalypse.

This picture, for which the artist used his blue palette, is done in gouache, watercolor, and pastel, with a wealth of modulations in both the warm and cool tones. The drawing has great power.

At times people used to accuse Rouault of indecency, because they could not see beneath the surface of his art to understand its meaning. "But without trying to impose on people or to erect a statue honoring myself," the painter wrote his friend Suarès, "I may permit myself to say that those who have taken thirty years to see, as they say today, the tooth marks of sin in my works—they are very blind."

Colorplate 12

CLOWN

c. 1907–8
Oil on paper, 23⅝ x 18½"
The Dumbarton Oaks Research Library and Collection,
Harvard University, Washington, D.C.
Robert Woods Bliss Collection

This is an example of the process of painting in oil and turpentine on paper that Rouault used in a number of his early pictures. The brush seems to say everything by suggestion, in a minimum of strokes, in a few touches, a few patches, without describing—I would even go so far as to say without *naming*—its subject too precisely. And the face is there before us, with a wit, an expressiveness, and even a bravado that astounds us. I admire the way Rouault notes the shyness of a look, the thickness of the lips, the pimpled flesh of a nose, the hollows of the cheeks. The clown places himself boldly, in complete self-awareness, before his fellowmen. He is a head in a ruff.

He is, as the expression goes, *craché*—spat out—onto the paper. But how many studies lie behind this apparent facility! How many persevering attempts there were before the achievement of this almost frenetic liberty! This clown appears before us, he speaks, he acts. His whole body is implied in his face. To evaluate this picture I shall employ a word I never use: it is a masterpiece.

Colorplate 13

ODALISQUE

1907

Watercolor, 25¼ x 38⅝"

Kunsthaus, Zurich. Bangerter Collection

Rouault gave the name Odalisque—derisively no doubt—to some of those in his series of "girls" or prostitutes. It is true, as her fan shows, that this one has about her a suggestion of a harem slave. The curve of her body has a special sensuosity that continues the rhythm established by her arms.

In January 1907 Manet's *Olympia*, after many battles, went from the Luxembourg Museum to the Louvre; it had created a great stir and obsessed many painters, beginning with Cézanne, who painted his *Modern Olympia* in 1873. As for Rouault, he gave the title *Olympia* to an Odalisque of 1905.

In order to fill the triangular space in the right foreground of this *Odalisque*, Rouault has placed an apple, like a reminder of Genesis, before this woman, with her serpentine forms. The overall color harmony is kept within the range of dark tones. To open up the space the artist has created a triangle of light tones in the background in which two girls are seated in Oriental fashion, gossiping.

Colorplate 14

THE WOMAN WITH THE BLACK GLOVE
1908

Gouache and watercolor
Private collection, Paris

Executed in Rouault's incomparable, inimitable style, this watercolor with gouache resembles some calligraphic flourish from the Far East, a fleeting vision composed of thick and thin strokes, hurled onto the paper like a confidence.

Everything is suggested here and requires some degree of collaboration from the viewer. And, little by little, it all becomes clear—the woman with her large hat, the little dog she asks to jump up on her knees—everything reveals itself to us like a note from a personal diary. But Rouault had about him nothing of an Amiel or a Félix Vallotton. He was not given to introspection. He did not search for himself beyond his own characteristic qualities.

The drawing is strong and the wash subtle; the accents are placed with a surpassing virtuosity that is employed only to better serve and express the idea.

A small work such as this demonstrates the spontaneity that replaced the academic skills Rouault had learned at the École but had now forgotten. One feels that the artist has no thought that his work may be seen by eyes other than his own. He does not come to meet us, but is there waiting for us. It is the rapid, unexpected, startling notation of his vision, with no concession made in his manner of seeing, that he maintains and, finally, imposes.

Colorplate 15

THE BARGE

1909

Watercolor and gouache, 22⅞ x 34⅝"
Musée de Peinture et de Sculpture, Grenoble

We have seen Rouault studying prostitutes and clowns; he was the first artist since Daumier whose vision had encompassed the disinherited and the vagabonds of the streets and the fairgrounds. Now to those tramps on the land he adds these vagabonds on the water, who ply their oars up and down the rivers.

The Barge is one of the few pictures (along with certain exodus images) in which Rouault shows his figures in an aquatic environment. Notice how he uses his cursive, violent, almost slashing drawing to give form to his invention. That elliptical way of tracing the contour of his figures in space—a contour that never ends, but is always in the process of becoming, of rotating—is something that he owes to Daumier and, perhaps even more, to Delacroix.

We see the boat moving down the stream. Seen close up, it is a series of comma-like accents, spontaneous and apparently imprecise. Seen from afar, everything falls into place, taking on face, body, expression. Observe how Rouault has rendered the water beneath the boat by a kind of scumbling, with gleams scratched into the surface, while farther off the water is calm. And see how the vertical of the barge's mast gives a certain stability to this gliding, balanced object as it floats between the two banks.

Colorplate 16

THE TRIBUNAL

c. 1910

Oil on canvas, 27⅝ x 42⅛"

Collection Mrs. Donald Stralem, New York

A friend of Rouault, Deputy Prosecutor Granier, took the artist to the Tribunal de la Seine to observe the court in session. In 1907, with his *Condemned Man,* the artist began a series of pictures of the people of the law courts—judges, lawyers, defendants. Thirsting for justice himself, Rouault was tormented by the need for an equitable distribution of truth among men.

In this painting everything takes place in a kind of subdued blue light; the scene is dominated, however, by the red robes of those who will pass judgment on others. The atmosphere is that of a bloodbath, and the head of the accused, at the right, seems to be the twin of that of the clerk, on the left. The lawyer, with his vindictive gaze, brandishes his notes.

Each of those paintings in which one feels all the relativity and inexactitude of a verdict—whether it is *The Accused,* the *Condemned Man,* or this *Tribunal*—is filled with Rouault's strong sense of drama. It seems that he is in turn each one of the participants in the trial whose atmosphere he evokes with his unique talent.

Colorplate 17

LANDSCAPE WITH DEAD TREES
c. 1913
Watercolor, gouache, and pastel, 7⅝ x 11¾"
Private collection, Paris

Every aspect of this watercolor, gouache, and pastel reflects a rare sensibility. This small picture evokes that recognition of human suffering that permeated Rouault's life. The two figures in the foreground are united with the houses of the village, the bell-tower, and the trunks of the dead trees, which thrust their verticals upward like a last gesture of hope before this landscape of desolation.

The work is executed with astonishing freedom, and the two small patches of white and pink made by the figures dominate the color harmony of this palette, which serves as the accompaniment to a moving and expressive drawing.

This is the prologue to the eternal exodus that was to become one of Rouault's enduring themes. Solitude, dialogue; in the whole village each house is as much like a person who tells his story—a story of poverty—as is the human figure in the foreground who bends toward the child in a pink smock.

"The mystery of plastic creation requires certain *skills*," wrote Rouault. "One does not simply improvise upon an emotion, even with a great sensibility . . . for a whole life of effort is also required." (Letter to André Suarès, from Versailles, August 10, 1913.)

At this time people were outraged by Rouault's painting. "Everyone is deserting me," he reported, "and I get insulting letters (I mean insulting to my art) from an old friend; it seems that people think I ask advice of the young people 'in the swim,' that I want to be modern, etc. . . ."

Colorplate 18

CHRIST MOCKED (PROFILE)
c. 1913
Oil on canvas, 28¾ x 23⅝"
Collection Jean Sawyer Weaver, Hillsborough, Calif.

In this work Rouault's painting, like that of all great artists—Tintoretto, El Greco, Rembrandt— is illuminated from *within*. Rouault shows not only a head, the head of Christ, but also—and above all—he evokes the experience that has shaped its appearance. The work proves what Van Gogh used to say: "One can give the impression of anguish without alluding directly to the historical garden of Gethsemane."

This work is imprinted with and completely dominated by all that is most precious; it brings tears to one's eyes and might even, it seems to me, transform one's life. As I look at this moving image, I think of what Léon Bloy wrote about the eyes of Christ, that their "deep blue is veiled by a sliding curtain of tears. These tears, two drops of light, do not yet overflow, but one sees that the eyelids are flooded with many more and will at any moment be unable to hold them back. . . . These eyes are moist and alive, not alive with an outward gaze but with a far more poignant and arresting gaze inward." (Letter to Georges Landry, from Périgueux, September 14, 1872.)

In 1942 Rouault painted a frontal, half-length *Christ Mocked* (colorplate 36) that is now in the Staatsgalerie, Stuttgart.

Colorplate 19

THREE CLOWNS

c. 1917

Oil on canvas, 41⅜ x 29½"

Collection Joseph Pulitzer, Jr., St. Louis

Here again it is the human family that Rouault presents to us, this time in these *Three Clowns* who are, in this oblique composition, almost a variation on his *Injured Clown* (colorplate 25). But in this work, whose figures seem to appear between two parted curtains, the painter seems to recall the three ages of man. One feels here more than anywhere else the wretchedness of those professional entertainers of the public, the men of the small circus—clowns, acrobats, and those who are called charlatans. In this work they become symbols of human suffering. Rouault charges even the smallest details of their gestures with tenderness and resignation. André Suarès wrote to him in 1917, "You see your buffoons and your simpletons as a lyric poet imagines the horror and misery of a landscape."

Nothing could be more true. Rouault possessed the art of making a facial expression—in this case that of the father, with his bent head—speak his own language, one which never strayed outside the range of visual possibility. And so he was not incorrect when he offered this definition of art, which contains in its brevity the whole mystery of art: "Form, color, harmony." These are the three pillars of his work, which he never failed to unite in his painting.

Colorplate 20

CHRIST IN THE SUBURBS

1920

Oil on canvas, 35⅞ x 28⅜"

Bridgestone Museum of Art, Tokyo

Rouault often referred to Belleville, the Parisian quarter where he grew up, and to the rue de la Villette, where he was born on May 27, 1871. Paris was then under the Commune, and counterrevolutionary troops were bombarding the north of Paris as they came in from Versailles, reconquering the city foot by foot.

"At the time when I lived there," the painter has said, "the old stud horses that pulled the small omnibus up the hill used to draw it along peacefully, setting the record for slowness, for the climb from the center of the town was a steep one. I would wander by day and by night from Belleville to Montmartre, almost too tired to stand. . . . In that old quarter I, like so many others, suffered many of those hardships which, although they may etch furrows and deep wrinkles on the face of the most beautiful girl, do not destroy people's courage or prevent the cobbler from singing."

It is there, in that poor people's quarter, that Rouault has placed his "suburbs of the prolonged sorrows." It is there also, in the center of working-class life, that his Christ appears—as he does here, in the midst of the sordid streets with their scrofulous children. A factory chimney rises in the background, the ground is swept by the rays of the moon; in the silence of the night the small procession slowly advances. Rouault's Christ has no need of a halo to identify Him. The painter has crowned Him with something very different from the false brilliance of gold: he has stamped Him with his own faith, with his own gratitude, and has shown Him as the greatest hope of suffering humanity. All this is communicated to us through the artist's hand, through the emotion that it has instilled in this paint, this pigment, that has been touched and worked, until its essence has been transfigured in this unforgettable creation.

Colorplate 21

CIRCUS TRIO (DANCERS AND PUNCH)

c. 1924

Oil on paper mounted on canvas, 29⅞ x 41¾"
The Phillips Collection, Washington, D.C.

Here we have an example of the grotesque side of Rouault's work. He often mocked human failings, but he never excluded himself from the black comedy in which we all, more or less, participate. This explains why, when one looks beneath the surface of his paintings, one recognizes that his formidable irony is always accompanied by a certain delicate intimacy, such as we see in this withdrawn and meditative Punch. Through a distortion in scale, Rouault has stressed the large head of his Punch, giving him an especially concentrated vigor in his place between the two dancers. The latter, who appear in profile, support him compassionately with a gesture that is, perhaps, a prefiguration of his *Injured Clown* of 1932 (colorplate 25).

The painting is dense, its substance distinctive, its coloring contained within the range of greens, blues, and ochers. The image is inscribed within a malicious circle of arms and hands in which the poor buffoon seems to be imprisoned.

I recall seeing this picture in Washington, D.C., among the works so discerningly collected by Duncan Phillips; there it offered a visual reply to Daumier's *Insurrection*.

The grotesque permitted Rouault's art to renew itself, preventing it from aging. As the painter said of himself in his *Souvenirs intimes,* he refused to "put on the cast-off clothing of the Past with the pretense of loving it . . . [or to] fossilize myself in the smile of the Gioconda."

Colorplate 22

PIERROT (PROFILE)
c. 1925
Oil on canvas, 25¼ x 18⅛"
Private collection, Switzerland

Here the painter's palette changes, the pigment acquires a powerful density. This profile, hacked out with a knife—or, rather, engraved like an intaglio—is that of the clown who without hypocrisy confesses that he wears makeup. It is our profile on our best days, for, as Rouault used to say, "Which one of us does not wear makeup?"

Built up out of a substance that seems almost granitic, this Pierrot, with his long upright neck, his strongly defined nostril, and his mouth ready with a quick retort, possesses a face in which each one of us can recognize himself; it is a face as it were *illuminated* by a gaze that contemplates human misery, a gaze softened by compassion. The profile stands out against a bare background intersected by a red-fringed curtain. The continuous, almost sculptured modeling of the beardless face, slightly purplish in the shaved areas, is emphasized by a strong outline.

This is a virile work that leaves an indelible impression on anyone who has seen it. Every aspect of the painting bears the mark of Rouault's strong personality, everything comes from deep within himself—the decisiveness of the line, the warmth of the color, the rough modeling of the tones against the background of green and blue slashed with mauve, the coldness of the white ruff.

On August 24th of this year Rouault wrote to Suarès: "I have ventured on colors that are more frank, hardly romantic at all—not very decorative either, in the sense in which the superficial proponents of design understand it, as if art were 'this' or 'that,' decorative or something else. . . ."

Colorplate 23

OLD CLOWN WITH WHITE DOG
c. 1925
Oil on canvas, 28¾ x 18⅞"
Private collection, Switzerland

This work represents a tragic moment in human life, that of old age. Rouault, who had read and reread Baudelaire, must have known of the passage in which the author of the *Petits poèmes en prose* draws a parallel between the "old man of letters who has outlived the generation he had brilliantly entertained" and the "poor circus performer, bent, worn-out, decrepit, a ruin of a man, leaning his back against one of the doorposts of his hut . . . whose booth the forgetful world no longer wants to visit."

Here we see the old showman seated, bending down toward his dog, his only remaining companion. But as always for Rouault, the tragedy is not played out in the situation, which is to him, after all, only the external reality. It is as a painter that Rouault succeeds in moving us, through his use of claret tones, intersected by a gray, a green, the yellow of the stool, the chalky white of the dog; through this arabesque of melancholic contours, and the actual substance of the pigments, which he has instilled with his commiseration and his sensibility as a visual poet.

"We are outcasts: my clowns are not so many *dispossessed kings;* their laughter is familiar to me, it comes close to unleashing the repressed tears that I feel, and it touches upon bitter resignation," Rouault wrote to Suarès in 1926.

Colorplate 24

FLEUR DU MAL

c. 1930
Gouache and oil, 16½ x 13⅜″
Private collection, Paris

In this gouache, made from Plate IV of his etchings of *Les Fleurs du Mal*, Rouault explored the savage aspect of this woman's face.

The picture is inspired by the poem called "La Beauté":

> *Je suis belle ô mortels! comme un rêve de pierre,*
> *Et mon sein, où chacun s'est meurtri tour à tour,*
> *Est fait pour inspirer au poète un amour*
> *Éternel et muet ainsi que la matière.*
>
> (I am fair, o mortals! like a dream of stone;
> My breast, where each has suffered in his turn,
> Is made to inspire the poet with a love
> Mute and eternal, like matter itself.)

This strongly outlined, violent profile, with its long neck, is surely an image of the radiant, self-assured cruelty that is sometimes called Beauty. But what is this beauty? Violence? Terror? The infinite? Ugliness? It is an ugliness that one cannot forget.

In Rouault's painting it is a woman, her profile outlined in black, with a white headdress and a yellow-orange flower in her hair. Hers is a sharp profile, as though it had been cut out with an axe.

The same theme was treated by Rodin, who was inspired by the same poem but interpreted it very differently, giving his image an eloquence that was not what Rouault found in Baudelaire. The painter saw instead this fascinating, impassive figure with her acute sharpness that is at once luminous and black.

Colorplate 25

THE INJURED CLOWN

1932

Oil on canvas, 78¾ x 47¼"

Private collection, Paris

This painting and *The Little Family* are the largest of Rouault's works. Looking at the broad forms, strongly inscribed in fiery colors, one can imagine what Rouault might have done had he ever been commissioned to do paintings that would cover large surfaces.

In 1927 I wrote: "We need a cardinal who would commission Rouault to do a huge *Triumph of Death,* like the one that was painted at Pisa. This artist would interpret this theme as a gruesome dance of all his prostitutes; the scarlet robes of his judges would pale under the red-hot forks of the demons; the angels would dispute the souls of his clowns; and up above, assembled in contemplation, would be the beautiful, transported figures of the *Miserere,* surrounding Christ, with His profound gaze, and imploring His holy charity."

It is the technique of this *Injured Clown* that reminds me of that wish, which I expressed when Rouault was fifty-six years old. Unquestionably, this great work shows how right it was to see in Rouault an artist worthy of decorating a chapel, as did Giotto and Masaccio in their time. But let us speak no more of that dream; it cannot be fulfilled, and the decorative splendor of the Church is thereby impoverished. Let us return instead to this circus of humanity that we see here in all its pathos. The strong diagonal expresses a sense of humility, of compassion, of brotherhood that struck me forcefully when, standing beneath this great picture, I conversed with the painter.

Mme. Cuttoli commissioned a tapestry based on this work from the Aubusson craftsmen.

THE HOLY COUNTENANCE
1933

Oil on canvas, 35⅞ x 25⅝"
Musée National d'Art Moderne, Paris

Rouault often treated the theme of the Holy Countenance. This painting was preceded by several earlier versions, among them the gouache in the Hahnloser collection (1912); one in a private collection in Zurich (1913); and the gouache, wash, and pastel (c. 1931) that is in Stockholm. The version reproduced here (which was presented to the museum by Mrs. Chester Dale, the wife of the great American collector) was followed by many other renderings of the Holy Countenance.

This rendition is quite poignant; the face emerges like a cry from the space in which it is painted. One has the impression that Rouault intended to show us the face of Christ coming to us across space and time. Around the face—to frame it, to give it a temporal context—he has painted a kind of jeweled casket made of colored gems.

Yet, if one must choose among Rouault's various renderings of this theme, it is *The Holy Countenance* of 1946, painted in tones of olive-brown and green, with deep black features, that seems to me the most overwhelming. There the artist succeeded in evoking the immortal aspect of a theme that only the greatest artists have treated with exceptional intuition.

Colorplate 27

THE MOUNT OF OLIVES
1930–36
Oil on canvas, 17⅜ x 13"
Private collection

This is one of a series of paintings executed by Rouault before the publication of *The Passion,* the collection of seventeen color etchings and eighty-two woodcuts, with an accompanying text by André Suarès, that Vollard published in 1939.

As he often did when beginning work on a graphic project, Rouault painted a series of subjects to be included in his book. Fifty-four of these oil paintings were shown in 1965 in an exhibition at the Galerie Charpentier in Paris. Among the most moving of these was *The Mount of Olives,* which shows Christ raising his hands toward heaven in supplication to His Father. Rouault has chosen the passage from The Gospel According to St. Luke in which the kneeling Son of Man, "being in an agony," is comforted by an angel (Luke 22:41–44).

Here Rouault's colors recall those of the old stained-glass windows that he restored as an apprentice. He uses his freshest palette, which is as resplendent as a bouquet of flowers.

"Everything you do is religious . . . ," Suarès wrote to him. "Your faith conceals itself because it is ardent. You have not made a profession of it, nor used it as a sign to attract the first comer."

IN THE OLD FAUBOURG (THE KITCHEN)

1937

Oil on canvas, 21⅝ x 27⅝"

Collection Julian J. and Joachim Jean Aberbach, New York

As one contemplates this kitchen scene, one thinks of "our daily bread," of the story of Mary and Martha, and of the intimacy of paintings by Chardin. There is great humility here, and a power to move us that derives from seeing a spiritual figure among the implements and objects of daily life.

The painter also achieves expressive power through his creation of a silence that emanates from his picture—a silence charged with meditation, a silence that gathers among the saucepans and around the pot and the kettle. This silence is accentuated by the reflection of the mysterious figure who sees Himself in the mirror. One would be ashamed to speak and thus break this calm in which time seems abolished and all hunger satisfied.

This profound image, conceived in broad planes, is in my opinion one of the most deeply religious works ever painted by Rouault. It reminds me of Valéry's phrase at the conclusion of his extraordinarily lucid description of the genesis of a work of art: "It is necessary to end with simplicity."

Colorplate 29

THE OLD KING

1937

Oil on canvas, 30¼ x 21¼"
Museum of Art, Carnegie Institute, Pittsburgh

I remember seeing a reproduction of Rouault's *The Old King* when I visited Matisse; it was pinned to the wall of his apartment in Cimiez, side by side with a color reproduction of a Van Gogh. "Look," Matisse said to me, "next to the Rouault, the Van Gogh looks like a painting from the eighteenth century."

It was true. Confronted with the assertive stature of *The Old King,* Van Gogh's work, boldly painted though it is, seems to dissolve into a kind of prettiness.

Looking at this virile image, one thinks of the Bible, of King David, of the remote past—of a man who will soon be going "the way of all flesh." It is one of the few works by Rouault that is filled with a somewhat legendary feeling, with the memory of Gustave Moreau. Yet the painting has nothing of the historical about it. It is carried out with singular power and authority, in a technique that in some places— the red of the clothing, the yellows of the crown and collar, the white of the bouquet of flowers—appears scarred, even as if it had been slapped on with the painter's hand. It is one of the most monumental works ever produced by the brush of an artist.

Colorplate 30

TWILIGHT

1937

Oil on canvas, 40 x 28½"
Collection Jacques Gelman, Mexico City

This landscape, which summarizes all of Rouault's compositions, is one of those in which the harmony between a landscape and a group of people rings most true. The scale and proportions are especially felicitous.

Under the vast, changeable sky, which seems to arch beneath a great wind, an assembly of people crowds around the white apparition of Christ. In the foreground two people are conversing. What are they saying? One senses that they are having a discussion in which they are not in complete agreement. Some question—possibly a crucial one—troubles them.

Yet in all this there is no trace of didactical painting, no hint of the philosophical art that Baudelaire described as having "pretensions to taking the place of words, that is to say, to competing with print as a teacher of history, morality, philosophy . . . ." There is no suggestion here of a "return to that imagery necessary during the childhood of a people, that monstrous imagery in which some fine talents have chosen to express themselves."

No, Rouault never betrayed his art. Observe how everything in this picture is resolved through color into a harmony of curves—those of the clouds in the sky and of the group of figures; curves that strike across the vertical forms of the tower, the men in the foreground, and the white apparition in their midst.

The image is searching, powerfully painted in a bold calligraphy unlike any other. Here Rouault's forceful personality reveals itself in every touch, every tone, every mark.

Colorplate 31

CRUCIFIXION
c. 1939
Oil on canvas, 25⅝ x 19¼"
Private collection, Paris

This is a theme that Rouault treated frequently, especially from 1918 to 1950. In the oil painting that we see here, his art has deepened noticeably since his first *Crucifixion*. In both pictures Rouault shows us the drama of the Cross on two levels: that of the historical event, a reminder of Christ's death in the presence of the Virgin and St. John; and that of Christ on the Cross, who seems to travel toward us, across space and time.

But while the composition of the early version—in spite of its admirable palette of subdued tones—still evokes some visual memory of Crucifixions painted by earlier masters, this one imposes itself on us by its originality. The arms of Christ are stretched out horizontally, and there is a marked separation between the dead body of Jesus and the resurrected face given to Him by Rouault.

The color is dominated by tones of slate and gold, with muted browns interspersed. There is one kneeling figure; the others stand. One would expect this to upset the balance of the composition and to distract our eyes from the essential element of the painting, the central figure of Christ. With one deep, almost black stroke on the left, however, the painter has reestablished the balance of his work, so that the face of Christ advances toward us, imposing itself on us by its verticality.

Colorplate 32

MOONLIGHT
c. 1940
Oil on canvas, 20½ x 15"
Private collection, Paris

This is one of the few pictures in which Rouault displays his cool palette. The design is broad, accentuated, established sometimes by strong verticals, sometimes by horizontals.

The range of colors, with its greenish tones interspersed with pink, blue, and white (as in the reflections in the water), is one we rarely encounter. Is this Christ and the fisherman? We do not know; we can only guess. Surely it is a religious elegy. The essence of the work lies in the white figure and His reflection, a Christ scarcely indicated—I would like to say scarcely named—yet filling the atmosphere of the painting with His presence.

We are far removed from Puvis de Chavannes's *The Poor Fisherman*. Here we are face to face with the *quintessence*. The healthy sweep of the drawing, achieved through a few astonishingly supple brushstrokes, makes the scene rise before us. The scene? No, for there is nothing dramatic about this picture. Quietly it places before us the painter, his talent, and his genius.

This is not the small landscape of one of those painters who are servile interpreters of natural scenes. "But these good *naturistes*," Rouault wrote to Suarès, "do you realize that they are as horrified by the word *caricature*, which you rightly refuse to apply to me, as by the word *nightmare*? These *naturistes*—at least most of them—are tied to the motif *Comme pendus à la corde/Ou chiens de garde à la chaîne* (Like hanged men to the rope/Or watchdogs to the chain)."

Colorplate 33

EQUESTRIENNE IN GRAY SKIRT
c. 1940
Oil and gouache, 14³/₁₆ x 10¹/₄″
Private collection, Paris

Rouault painted a series of equestriennes, beginning with the half-length version of 1906 in the Musée d'Art Moderne de la Ville de Paris. There is also a gouache of about 1932, painted in olive tones. In it the equestrienne on horseback is shown in profile, as she is in the lithograph of 1925–27, with its velvety blacks, and in the picture reproduced here, one of the latest in date.

This work is painted in a range of colors that goes from blue to gray, from brownish red to pinkish white, from the orange of the plume to copper yellow.

Scrupulous observation has taught the painter to understand the movement of the horse's hooves as it passes by with the high-style, almost mechanical step learned in training. And nothing is required of the equestrienne but to be on parade. Painted in oil and gouache, the whole scene is represented in profile, like a procession from the Parthenon frieze.

Colorplate 34

VERSAILLES (THE TERRACE)

c. 1940

Oil and gouache, 18½ x 29½"

Georges Rouault Studio, Paris

This picture in gouache and oil is somewhat unusual in Rouault's work. It is a painting in which everything is simply sketched in—one in which, nevertheless, everything is said. Distinguished chiefly by its technique, its rapid calligraphy and bold strokes are like stabs of the stiletto.

This is a light Rouault, with its delicate tones ranging between brownish mauve and cerulean blue. For the painter, it is a study in the relationship of three tones: mauve, blue, and pink.

Notice how he sets the scene, how he evokes lively attitudes among the coldness of the sculptures and balustrades, the lake and the distant horizon. The handling is airy, concentrated, punctuated by assertive brushstrokes. This painting is like a page from the painter's private diary that shows us how to forget everything, how to forget even what one has learned, in order to listen only to one's own sensations, one's own heart and vision.

"The taste for fine distinctions of quality is a joy to the eye and the spirit," said Rouault, "but to have it is also like dragging with one the iron ball of a convict."

Colorplate 36

CHRIST MOCKED

Completed 1942
Oil on canvas, 41½ x 29¾″
Staatsgalerie, Stuttgart

I recall seeing this picture in Cannes during World War II. It was left in the back of a shop, as if it had been abandoned there. And yet, in those troubled times, it seemed to be a sign of hope and resurrection. I was told some foolish stories about it—the kinds of thing dealers sometimes invent in order to create colorful anecdotes about a painting that could manage very well without them.

This is one of the most moving examples in all religious painting. Since Rembrandt's *Ecce Homo,* I know of no other work that brings us so directly into the presence of Christ, whose Passion is recalled in every element of the painting. He is the world's victim and its conqueror. Rouault shows Him full face, in that pigment so distinctively worked, every touch of which seems to be the result of an inner struggle.

This is the man! And every day, at every moment, the fact is repeated—within us and outside of history, at no fixed date, in no fixed place, with no possibility of containing it within the space and time across which it passes.

Colorplate 37

DECORATIVE FLOWERS

c. 1942

Oil on canvas, 13¾ x 10⅜"

Private collection

Bouquets are rather rare in Rouault's work. This one is distinguished by its colors. Here the dominant yellows replace the carmine reds and brownish greens that he more frequently stressed. The warm grays of the border surround the flowers and give this still life the resonance of a minor key.

Looking at this work, we are struck by its spontaneity. It is made up of a mass of subtle tones against which the yellow flowers and vase are juxtaposed. The whole work seems dashed off like a brush drawing, which gives the painting its touch, its significance.

This picture is an interesting example of Rouault's technique. It reveals the authoritative calligraphy that had already appeared in the oils and watercolors of 1905.

Colorplate 38

BLUE PIERROTS
c. 1943
Oil on canvas, 23¼ x 17¾"
Private collection, Paris

At the top of a stairway with brownish-pink steps (possibly at Versailles), a tall and a short Pierrot stand between two urns containing bouquets of flowers. Another nocturne, this is a clash of cymbals in the night. One is seduced by the dreamlike blues, by the enchantment of the spectacle—for that is what it is.

The technique is free, in some places emphatic. Sometimes it is a band of color that dominates; sometimes the accentuated drawing as it reveals the outline. This leitmotiv appears throughout Rouault's work, circumscribing all the Pierrots that he painted from all possible angles—full face, in profile—and in all kinds of surroundings.

These Pierrots are nocturnal apparitions, travelers whose humanity is without falsehood, characters in the human comedy of which they are the eternal victims.

Colorplate 39

VERONICA

c. 1945

Oil on canvas, 19⅝ x 14⅛″

Private collection, Paris

Rouault, painter of the Holy Countenance, never lost interest in this legendary saint who was seized with compassion when she saw Christ on the road to Calvary. Seeing His face streaming with sweat and blood, she wiped it with a piece of linen, which kept the imprint of His face. Rouault must have been thinking of her when he painted his group of holy women for the Prix de Rome competition.

Like the man born blind in the Reims Passion play, Rouault might have said:

Veronne, doulce créature,
Vous devez être bien joyeuse
Quand Dieu vous a fait si heureuse
De sa très digne face empreindre
En votre queuvre-chef.

(Gentle creature, Veronica,
You must have felt great joy
When God Himself made you so happy,
Imprinting the scarf from your head
With His most noble countenance.)

Here it is Veronica's face that Rouault presents to us as a symbol of compassion. He shows her with her expression of special sensibility; he shows her as the one who understands, who ministers, who forgives. Hers is the true face of kindness; the face that, astonished by nothing, is yet moved by everything, asking of man no more than he can give.

He has surrounded this face with veils—this face with its dull complexion, its delicate oval, its almost weeping eyes, its mouth that is ready to console without speaking a single word. Rouault has made her, with his unusual blues and the brown of the flesh, a mirror of the walk to Calvary.

Colorplate 40

THE FLIGHT INTO EGYPT I

c. 1945
Oil on canvas, 24 x 18½"
Private collection, Paris

In the homogeneous whole the pigment, the color, and the light form an ensemble of inseparable elements. We see here how Rouault uses color to establish the hierarchical order of his composition. Pictorially speaking, everything is of equal value, although the principal accents are placed on the white of the Virgin; on Joseph, who holds the horse's bridle; and on the orange moon. Our eyes then pass to the buildings and to the blue bands of the landscape. It would be impossible, however, to isolate the figures in the foreground without weakening them. The expanse of the ground, the towers, and the vast sky veritably make them *breathe,* giving them all the solidity that they need.

Like Rembrandt, Rouault frequently painted night scenes. Though he lived during the period of Post-Impressionism, when many painters, following the example of Seurat, were still seeking to render the vibrations of light, he boldly turned to the colors of that night palette that only the most powerful painters can use.

Here again Rouault was attracted to an episode in the childhood of Christ that forms part of that unending flight, that exodus on the road, that migration that haunted the artist. His intuition warned him not to rest in the comfortable security of order, which is in truth only a premonition of death. He always regarded life as an encampment in a temporary hostelry.

Colorplate 41

CHURCH INTERIOR

1945

Oil on canvas, 24 x 18½"

Private collection, Paris

After *The Child Jesus Among the Doctors,* Rouault had painted very few interiors of religious buildings. This one is punctuated with broad patches of color. It is as if, in this case, the artist were modestly refraining from showing us the congregation in the church; he simply breaks the silence and suggests the crowd's presence by means of these three figures, who seem to whisper among themselves, in the foreground.

The interludes of color are presented with facet-like brilliance. Beneath the dark green vaulting Rouault has delighted in evoking the radiance of the stained-glass windows, which reminded him of his apprenticeship when he restored stained glass with Tamoni. "Dear men of the past, far removed from the spirit of commercialism," he wrote, "I dreamed of being your servant and used to conjure you up by shutting my eyes."

The work is broadly painted, with a meditative silence attained through the arrangement of the objects and planes on the canvas. Two touches of madder red on the choirboys in the foreground suffice to open out the space.

Rouault painted two other pictures with this same theme in which the viewpoint is panoramic and includes a large congregation.

Colorplate 42

FLOWERS AND FRUIT
1946
Oil on canvas, 14⅝ x 10¼"
Private collection, Paris

The space is suggested through the building up of planes; the tones are both pure and refined. The white of the napkins forms a base underneath the fruit, while above the fruit the vase and the flowers have a compact density.

In this picture there is no repetition—no regular serpentine curve, no rectangle, no oval is repeated. To me this is Rouault's most important treatment of still life, a subject not often found in his work.

The outlines in this picture are irregular; each one is shaded by the artist's sensibility. The modulation of the colors is extremely delicate. Everything is in place—one could not move a fruit or a flower without disturbing the balance of the entire arrangement.

Colorplate 43

AUTUMN

c. 1946

Oil on canvas, 18½ x 13⅜"

Private collection, Paris

The mother, carrying her burden, crosses the road with her two daughters, one of whom has a basket on her arm. This is a nocturnal scene of brown tones and subdued greens in which the star of lemon cadmium is the only source of light.

The two figures in the middle distance are almost indistinguishable from the road and the ground. But in the foreground the procession of suffering women is like a frieze. It is the procession of the humble, of those who *do not know,* of those who pay for the others, of those who spend their lives in the acceptance of their tormenting labors.

One can distinguish within the composition, as if they have been pasted on, the white of a head scarf, the tuft of a tree. The opposing lines play harmoniously within the oblique composition.

Rouault never believed in painting noble subjects. He confided to Suarès, "As in the past, when I looked at fairground parades or, at the age of fourteen, admired the old stained-glass windows, forgetting everything, including myself, I discovered this primary truth—a tree against the sky has the same character and the same expressiveness as the human figure. It is a question of saying it. The difficulty begins there."

Colorplate 44

BLUE PIERROTS WITH RED FLOWERS
c. 1946
Oil on canvas, 14 x 10⅜"
Private collection, Paris

Two Pierrots—one tall, one short—stand face to face, separated by a large bouquet of flowers. The extraordinarily substantial whites stand out against the blue-green background, which is intersected by violet tones. Against the background and the forms outlined in blue, the flowers strike a note of sumptuousness—but it is a sumptuousness that does not exclude a suggestion of the redness of blood.

The painting has a distinctive flavor, and the density of the pigment is exceptional. To appreciate this oil painting, one must look at it from a distance. It is one of those studio works that shows Rouault's method of painting with broad touches of impasto, carefully placed to articulate his forms. There is harmony here, together with the nocturnal side of Rouault's painting that revealed itself at this time. The painting is alive, vibrant.

From the first glance I was impressed by the painterly quality of this picture. My eyes perceived in it a shimmering light like that of precious stones; at the same time, the chilled, almost frightening tones of the background and of the two Pierrots evoked a strong sense of tragedy.

Colorplate 45

TERESINA

1947

Oil on canvas, 20⅛ x 13¾"
Private collection, Paris

Beginning in 1947, Rouault painted a series of faces viewed close-up, as in this example. These faces are so vibrantly alive that they suggest biblical characters appearing beneath the main tent of the circus. The characterizations are pushed to the point of suggesting types, sometimes of a grotesque fashion, sometimes of circus performers or legendary figures.

Until about 1956 these close-ups (full face, three-quarters face, profile) were the occasions for festive outbursts of color, making this period one of the most brilliant in Rouault's entire career. A woman's face, as was so often the case with his clowns, was only a pretext for the joy of painting.

Teresina has her crown, whether of gold or of cardboard does not matter. Her huge eyes, glancing sideways, tell us that she is listening to something which, to judge from the expression of her mouth, does not seem completely convincing.

The technique is Rouault's usual one. The form of the face is circumscribed by a thick outline within which the color blends into a continuous modeled surface. Rouault's *Teresina* reminds me of the portraits on the ancient Christian mummies from the Fayoum district in lower Egypt. She has the same facial expression, the same intensity of gaze, the same monumental quality.

Colorplate 46

HOMO HOMINI LUPUS
1948
Oil on canvas, 18⅛ x 25⅝"
Musee National d'Art Moderne, Paris

As is evident in his clowns and biblical landscapes, Rouault's individuality is so strong and pervasive that it is rarely possible to compare one of his paintings with a work by one of his predecessors. Here, however, in this evocation of disaster, his hanged man does remind one of the hanged man of the *Disasters of War,* even though neither his technique nor his presentation is like that of Goya.

Homo Homini Lupus—man is a wolf to his fellowman. For all their differences, what unites these two renderings of the same subject is the horror of war that they both inspire. In Goya's work, the officer with his elbow resting on a stone contemplates his victim with satisfaction. In that of Rouault, only the burning houses of a village accompany the poor devil who hangs from a gibbet.

In this tragic atmosphere with its bloodstained moon, the white of the shirt of Rouault's hanged man, the innocent victim of men who have turned torturers, somehow introduces a mysterious feeling of resurrection.

Colorplate 47

BIBLICAL LANDSCAPE
c. 1949
Oil on canvas, 13 x 17¾"
Private collection, Paris

This is a dense, encrusted work, offering a kind of spiritual nourishment for the eyes. This kneaded, ground-up, whipped impasto, this strongly applied and subtly modulated color, is firmly held within a thick line that is encircled by a matrix of precious colors. One feels here the hand, the heart, and the mind of a visionary who has not bothered to determine where the workman's labor ends and that of the artist begins, for in his work the two professions, the manual and the spiritual, are indivisible.

In consequence, this biblical scene, brought before us through these pure and strictly painterly qualities, scarcely requires the commentary that such a subject would usually demand.

Every time I visit the house that belonged to the artist—the house where this picture stands on an easel in the same room as the massive table at which I used to sit and talk with Rouault—I always look at this work, and I am vividly reminded of his touch, his talent, and even of his faith. In this picture nothing is emphasized, yet, by suggestion, everything is said within its modest dimensions. Looking at it, I recall the words, often quoted by Rouault, of one of his great predecessors: "Genius does not lie in the format."

THE FLIGHT INTO EGYPT II

1952

Oil on canvas, 14⅝ x 13"

Private collection, Paris

In this late work the pigment has become volcanic; it is like a thick crust under pressure from an internal fire. Rouault had spoken to me of the illumination that arises from Rembrandt's "mud." Here the light emanates from a substance reminiscent of that of which meteors are formed: it is, one feels, in a state of fusion.

This oil painting reveals the Oriental side of Rouault who, like Goethe and all great artists, encompassed within himself the opposite poles of human nature. The drawing, echoed again and again in the reds, Veronese greens, and old golds, resolves finally into a few strongly affirmed accents that conjure up the forms and figures in all their monumentality. The surface has astonishing relief effects; a veritable embossing breaks the picture plane, giving it an extraordinary shimmer and density.

But how much work all of this has cost! As Rouault said, "I have managed to be a 'convict' for part of my life, and to be caught in the nets of necessity without deviating from a certain inner line or selling my inalienable spiritual liberty, the only possession I truly believe in."

SELECTED BIBLIOGRAPHY

BOOKS ILLUSTRATED BY ROUAULT

Arland, Marcel. *Les Carnets de Gilbert*. Paris, 1931 (with one original lithograph and 5 color engravings).

Rouault, Georges. *Le Cirque de l'étoile filante*. Paris, 1938; printer's date March 5, 1936 (with 17 etchings in color and 82 wood-engravings).

———. *Divertissement*. Paris, 1943 (with 15 color reproductions).

———. *Miserere*. Paris, 1948 (with 58 etchings).

———. *Miserere*. Preface by the artist. Introduction by Monroe Wheeler. New York, 1952 (small facsimile of 1948 edition).

———. *Miserere*. Preface by the artist. Introduction by Anthony Blunt. Foreword by Isabelle Rouault. Translation by Arnold Fawcus. Boston and Clairvaux, 1963 (small facsimile of 1948 edition).

———. *Paysages légendaires*. Paris, 1929 (with 6 tipped-in lithographs and 50 drawings, one lithograph in color for the first 12 copies).

———. *Petite Banlieue*. Paris, 1929 (with 6 lithographs and 100 reproductions, 2 hand-colored by the artist).

———. *Soliloques*. Preface by Claude Roulet. Neuchâtel, 1944 (with 8 color reproductions).

———. *Souvenirs intimes*. Paris, 1926 (with 6 tipped-in lithographs).

———. *Stella Vespertina*. Paris, 1947 (with 12 color reproductions).

Suarès, André. *Passion*. Paris, 1939 (with 17 etchings in color and 82 wood-engravings).

Vollard, Ambroise. *Les Réincarnations du Père Ubu*. Paris, 1932 (with 22 etchings and 104 wood-engravings).

WRITINGS BY THE ARTIST

Georges Rouault—André Suarès: Correspondence. Introduction by Marcel Arland. Paris, 1960.

Sur l'art et sur la vie. Preface by Bernard Dorival. Paris, 1971 (includes text of *Soliloques* and the artist's collected essays on painters and art, poems, and letters).

WRITINGS ON ROUAULT

Bellini, Paolo. *Georges Rouault: Uomo e artista*. Milan, 1972.

Brion, Marcel. *Georges Rouault*. Paris, 1950.

Charensol, Georges. *Georges Rouault, l'homme et l'oeuvre*. Paris, 1926.

Cogniat, Raymond. *Georges Rouault*. Paris, c. 1930.

Courthion, Pierre. *Georges Rouault*. Catalogue of works prepared with the collaboration of Isabelle Rouault. New York, 1962.

Dorival, Bernard. *Cinq Études sur Georges Rouault*. Paris, 1957.

———. *Rouault*. Paris, 1963.

Dyrness, William A. *Rouault: A Vision of Suffering and Salvation*. Grand Rapids, 1971.

George, Waldemar (pseud.), and Nouaille-Rouault, Geneviève. *Georges Rouault: Aquerelles*. Paris, 1971.

———. *L'Univers de Rouault*. Paris, 1971.

Homage to Georges Rouault. Special issue of *XXᵉ Siècle*. Edited by G. di San Lazzaro. Translated by Joan Sanchez. New York, 1971.

Jewell, Edward Alden. *Georges Rouault*. New York, 1945.

Lassaigne, Jacques. *Rouault*. Geneva and New York, n.d. (1951?).

Marchiori, Giuseppe. *Rouault*. New York, n.d.

Maritain, Jacques. *Georges Rouault*. New York, 1952.

New York. Museum of Modern Art. *Georges Rouault: Paintings and Prints*. Text by James T. Soby. 3rd ed., New York, 1947. Exhibition catalogue.

———. *Rouault: Retrospective Exhibition*. New York, 1953. Exhibition catalogue.

Paris. Musée National d'Art Moderne. *Georges Rouault: Exposition du Centenaire*. Paris, 1971. Exhibition catalogue.

Paris. Musée du Louvre. *Georges Rouault: Oeuvres inachevées données a l'État*. Text by Bernard Dorival. Paris, 1964. Exhibition catalogue.

Puy, Michel. *Georges Rouault*. Paris, 1921.

Roulet, Claude. *Rouault: Souvenirs*. Neuchâtel and Paris, 1961.

Venturi, Lionello. *Georges Rouault*. New York, 1940. 2nd ed., Paris, 1948.

———. *Rouault: Biographical and Critical Study*. Lausanne, 1959.

Wotsky, Alan. *Georges Rouault: The Graphic Work*. London and San Francisco, 1976.

INDEX

PHOTOGRAPH CREDITS

Basnier, Paris; Bernheim-Jeune, Paris; Bijtebier, Brussels; Bing, Paris; Caillet, Paris; Galerie Louis Carré, Paris; Yvonne Chevalier, Paris; Doisneau, Paris; Drayer, Zurich; Fortier, Paris; Giraudon, Paris; Hurault, Paris; Nelson, New York; Savonnet, Paris; Tooth, London; Marc Vaux, Paris; Vizzavona, Paris; Vollard, Paris; Weill, Paris